THE INSPIRATIONAL TRAVEL QUOTES BOOK

160+ ORIGINAL TRAVEL AND INSPIRATIONAL QUOTES IN COLOR

AVENTURAS DE VIAJE

Graphics by
RACHEL PASTORES

Copyright Aventuras De Viaje © 2018

www.SurvivalFitnessPlan.com

All rights reserved
No part of this document may be reproduced without written consent from the author.

All quotes are Bert Luxing originals and are protected by common copyright law.

All images are in public domain.

Bert Luxing is a minimalist world traveler, so-so entrepreneur, my unofficial mentor, and most importantly, a lifelong friend.

The quotes in this book are ones I have heard him say at some stage during our conversations.

There are many gems of wisdom, most of which have spilled out of his mouth during the normal course of conversation.

There are also some where he was reciting someone else's quote but clearly got it wrong. They are great none the less.

I hope you can continue to enjoy them as much as I do.

CONTENTS

160+ Travel and Inspirational Quotes	1
Afterword	173
Author Recommendations	175
About the Author	177

A life of travel is one you'll never want to escape from.

Life is to be lived.

The world is only black and white until you fill it with your own color.

AVENTURAS DE VIAJE

The best way to truly learn what the world has to offer is to travel.

There's nothing stopping you from living a never-ending adventure.

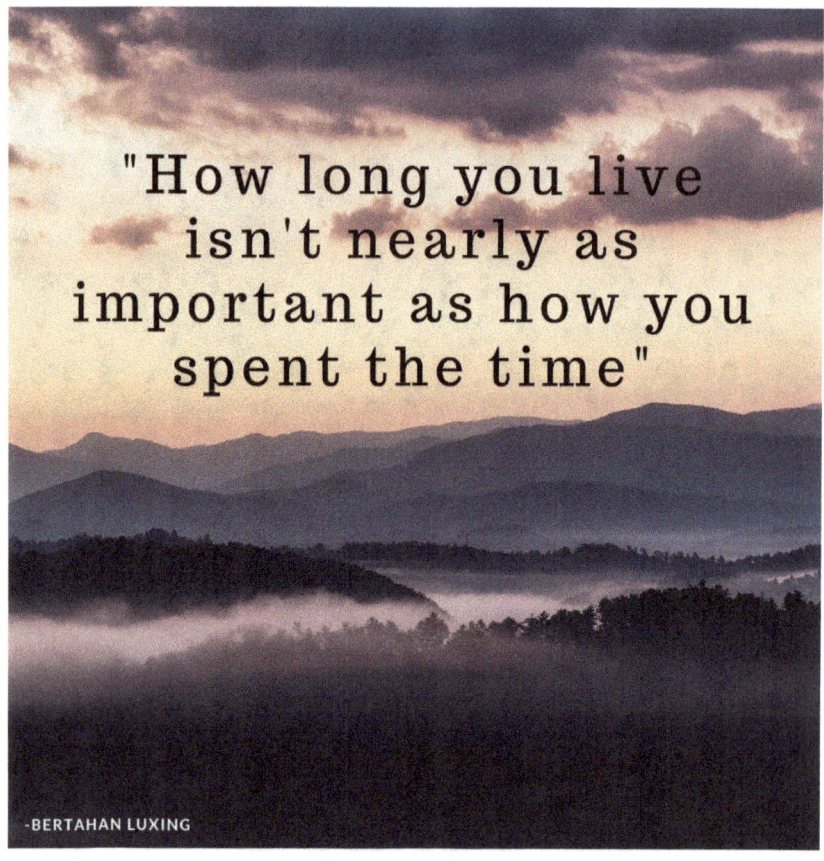

How long you live isn't nearly as important as how you spent the time.

Working for the weekend is no way to live. Every day is a weekend for the traveler.

Make the most of what you have. So many have much less.

Don't wait for life to happen, because before you know it you'll have waited too long.

Nothing is a waste of time if you are enjoying yourself.

There's so much beauty in the world, everyone should see at least some of it.

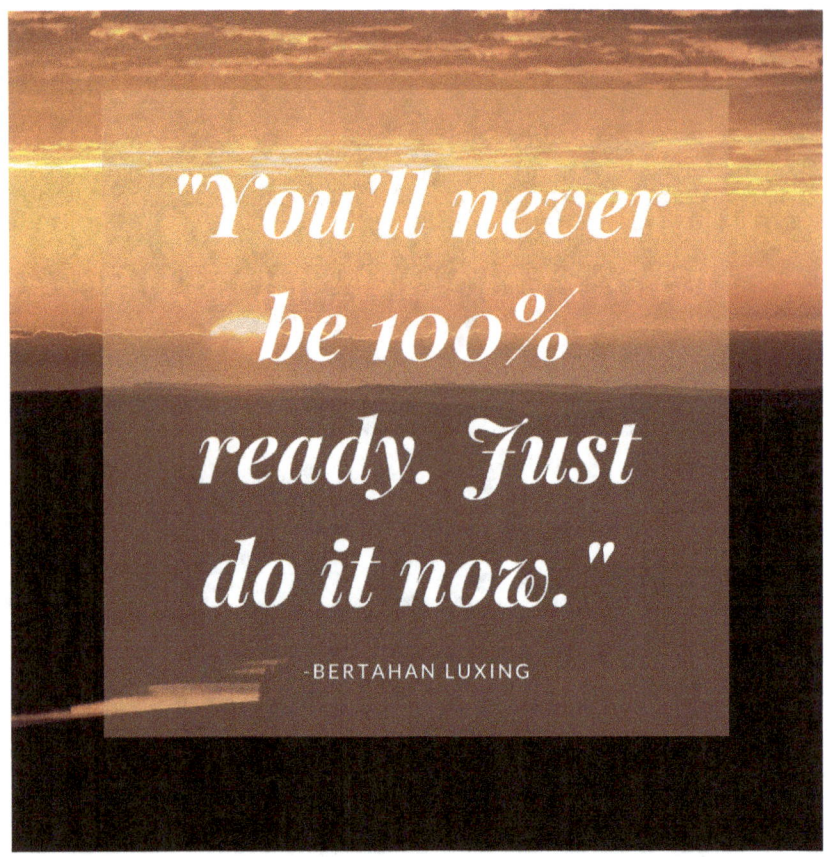

You'll never be 100% ready. Just do it now.

Travel will teach you things no school ever could.

It's up to you to make the best life you can.

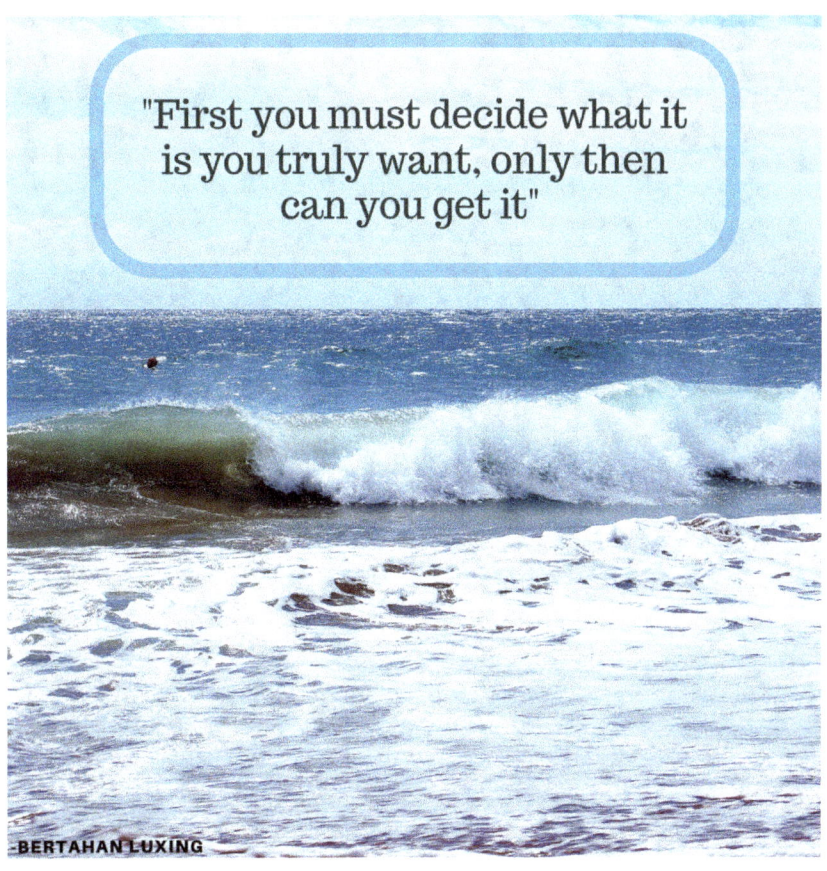

First you must decide what it is you truly want, only then can you get it.

Go out there and learn about the world from experience.

More stuff won't make you happier. Enjoy what you have.

There is no need to conform to social norms if you don't want to. Break free.

Those who are curious about the world will see much more of it.

When you travel you not only see new things, you will see old things new.

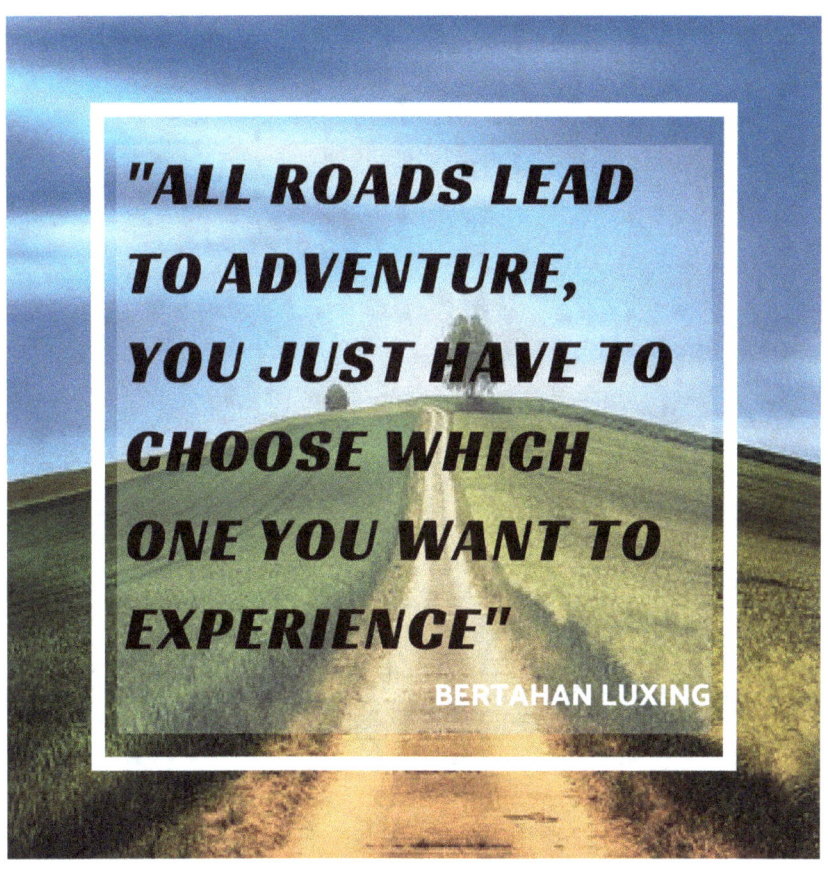

All roads lead to adventure, you just have to choose which one you want to experience.

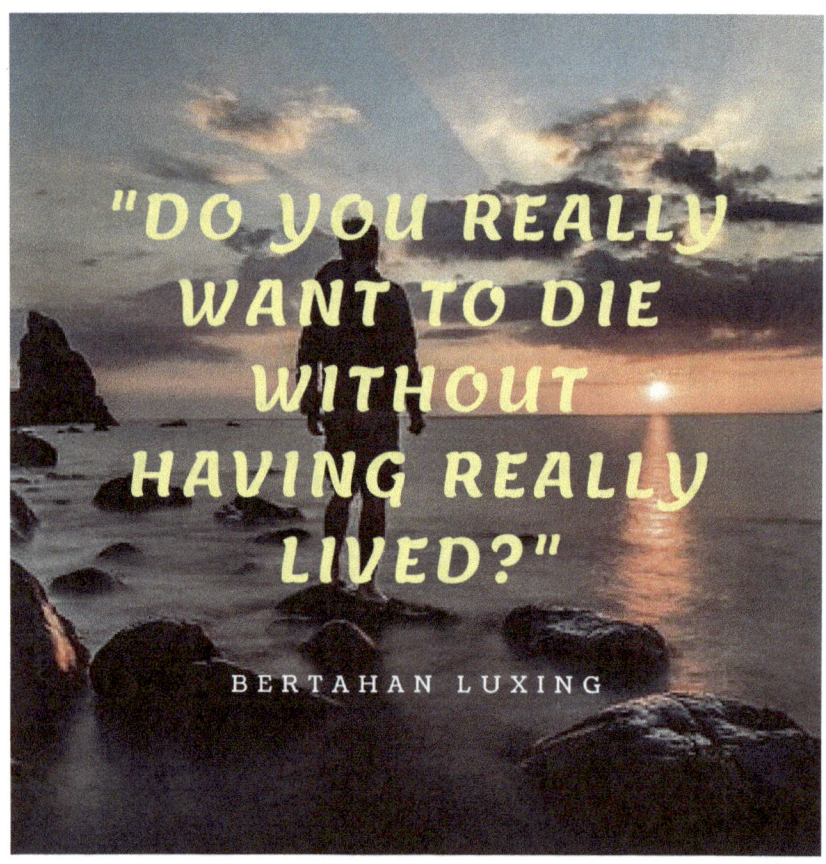

Do you really want to die without having really lived?

I much prefer seeing the same nature than seeing the same concrete.

If you get homesick, look at the moon. It's always the same one no matter where you are, for Earth is your home.

It's up to you to discover how far you can go.

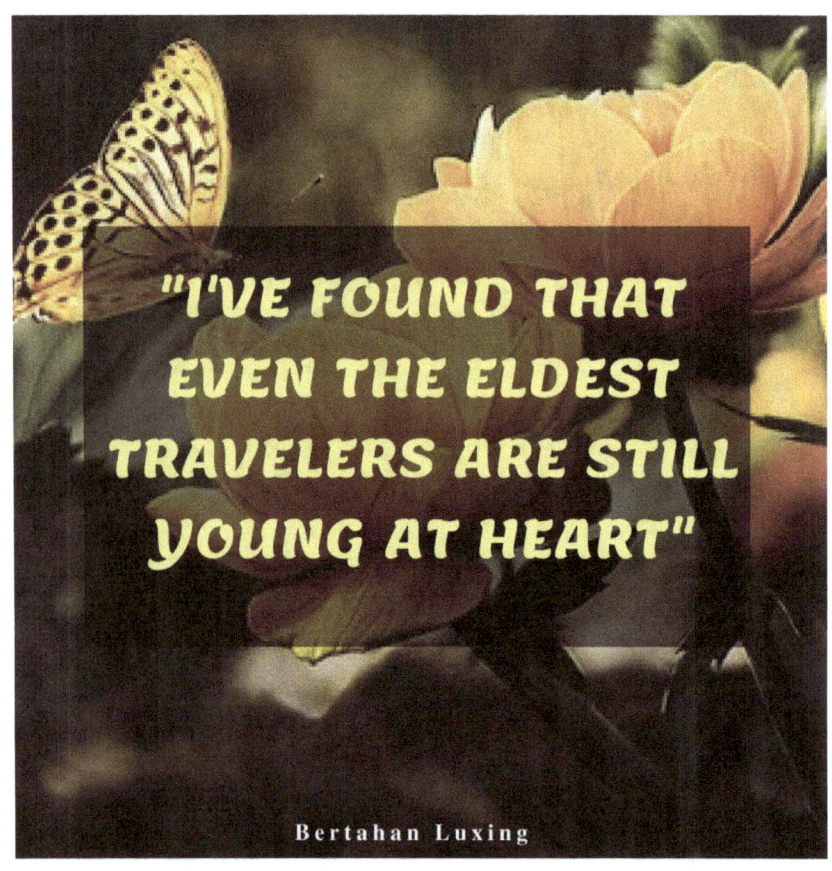

I've found that even the eldest travelers are still young at heart.

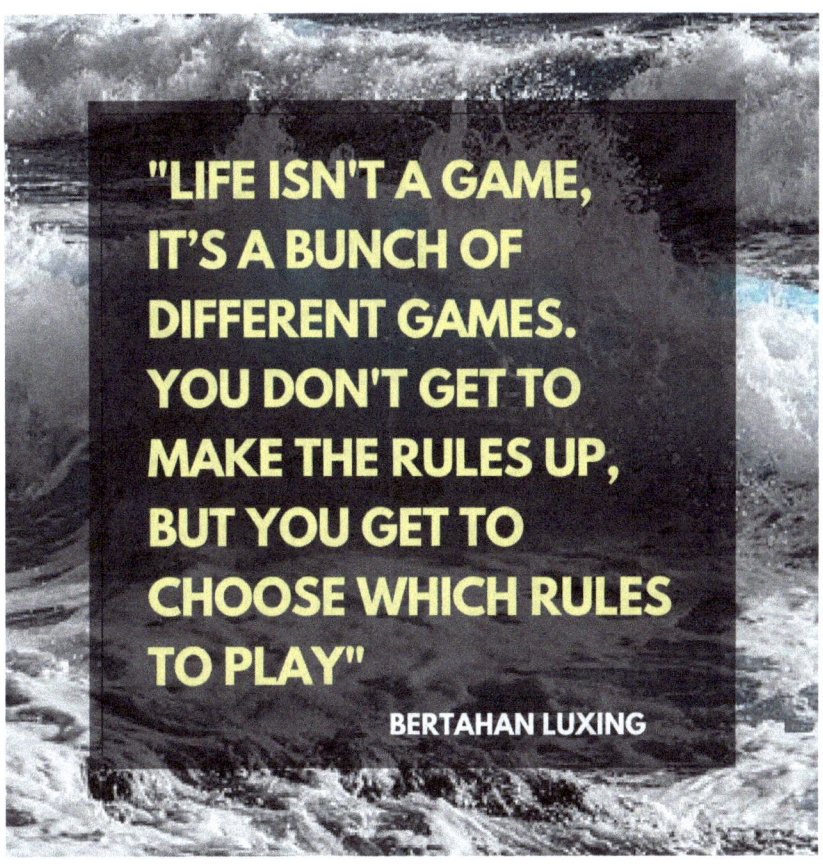

Life isn't a game, it's a bunch of different games. You don't get to make the rules up, but you get to choose which rules to play.

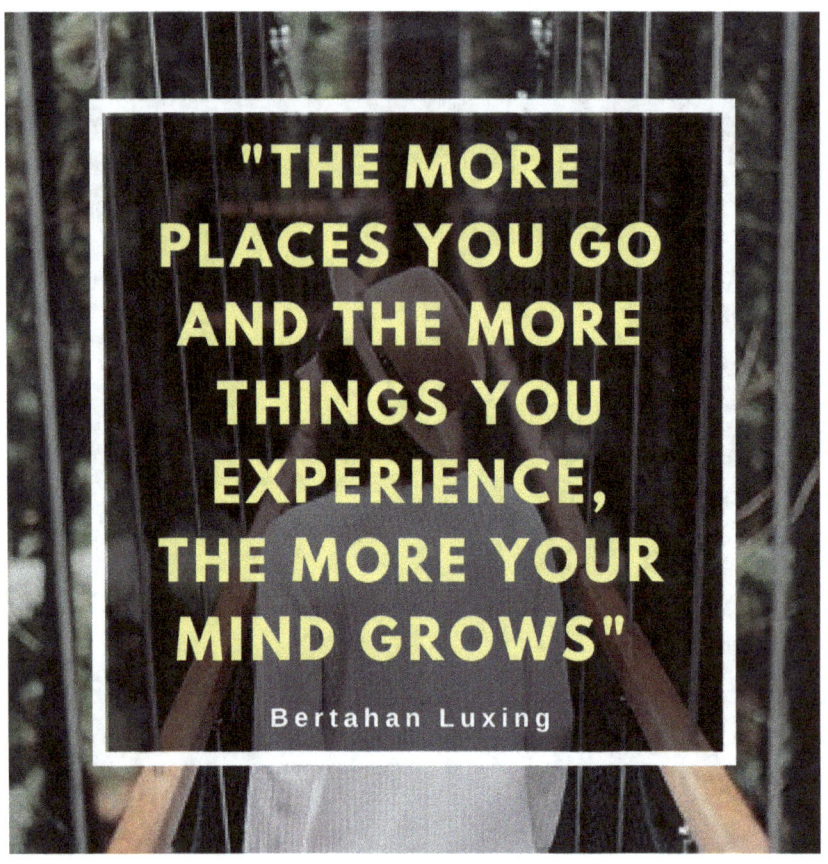

The more places you go and the more things you experience, the more your mind grows.

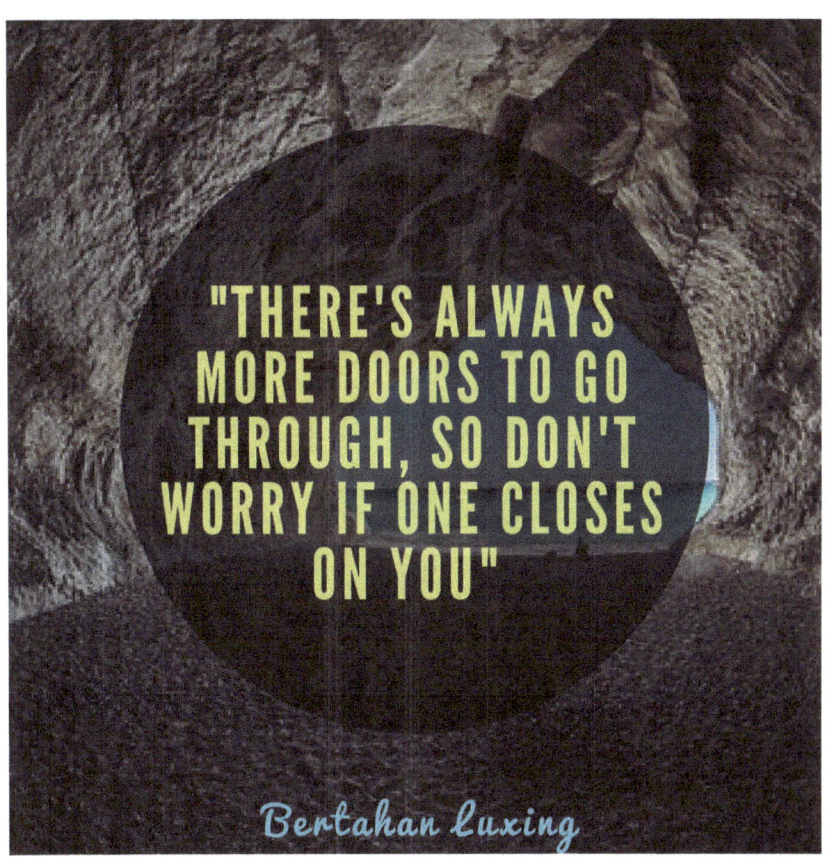

There's always more doors to go through, so don't worry if one closes on you.

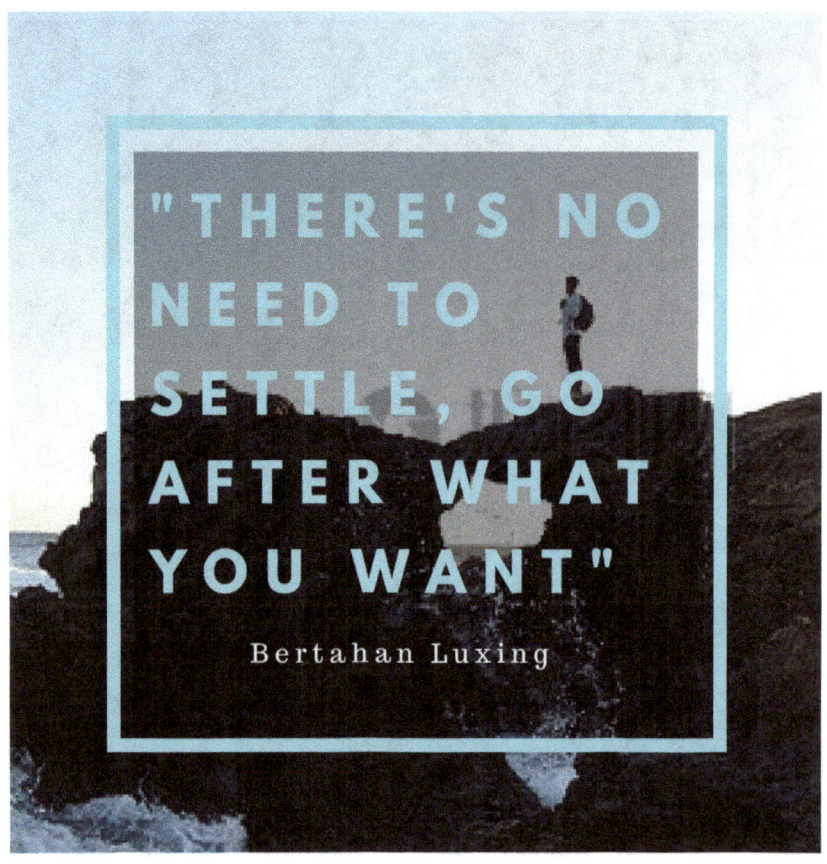

There's no need to settle, go after what you want.

Unfocused travel is one of the best teachers of life lessons.

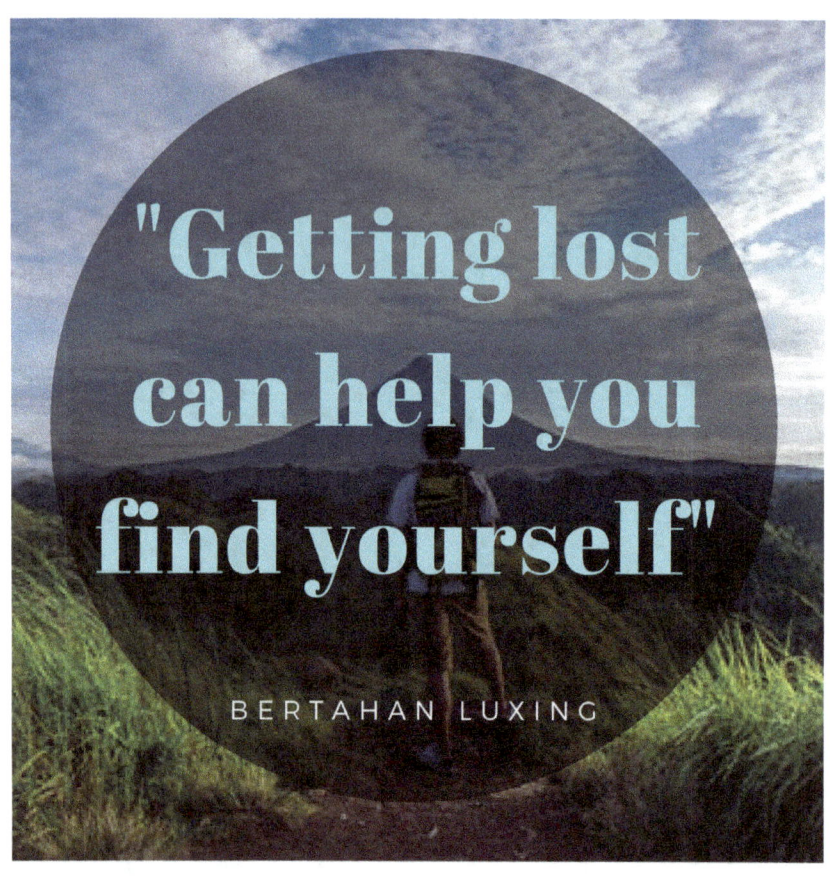

Getting lost can help you find yourself.

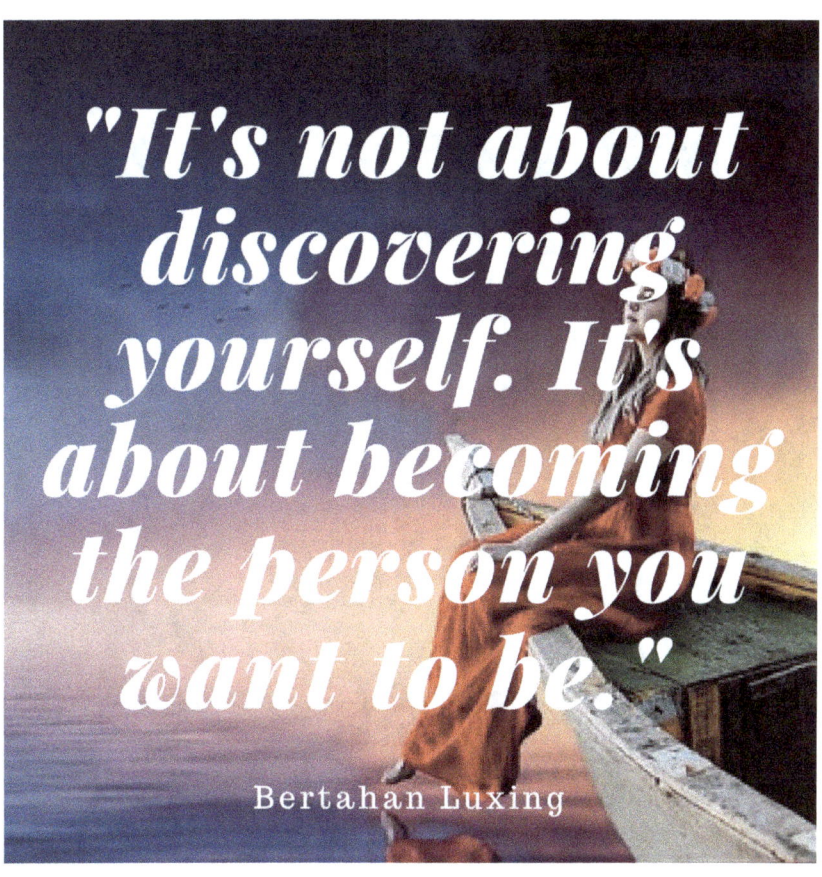

It's not about discovering yourself. It's about becoming the person you want to be.

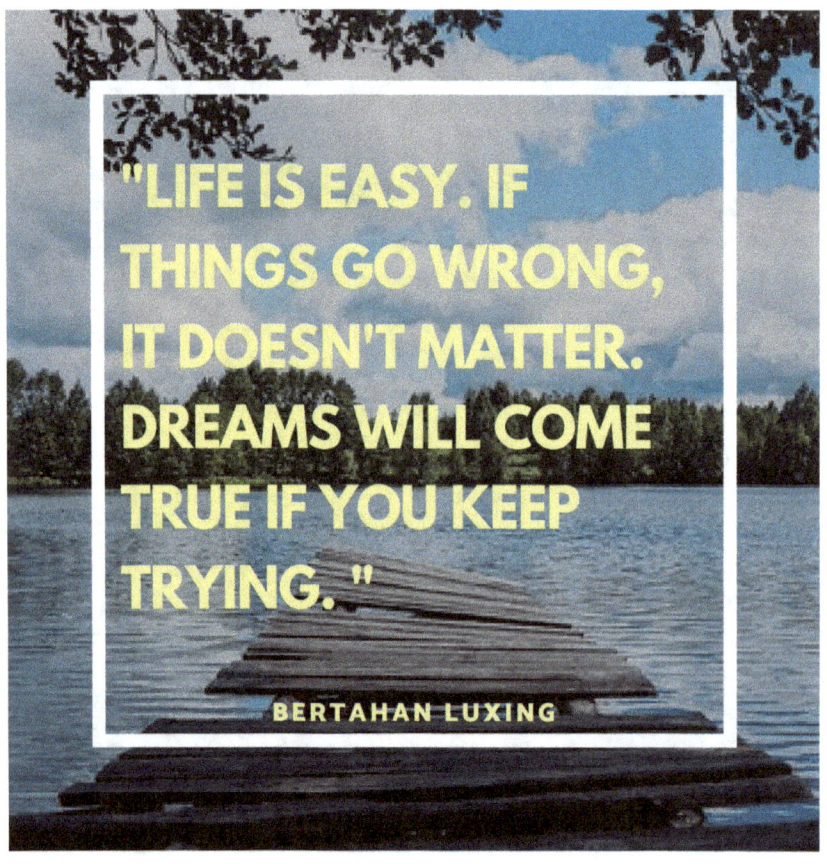

Life is easy. If things go wrong it doesn't matter. Dreams will come true if you keep trying.

Use your time wisely. Experience life.

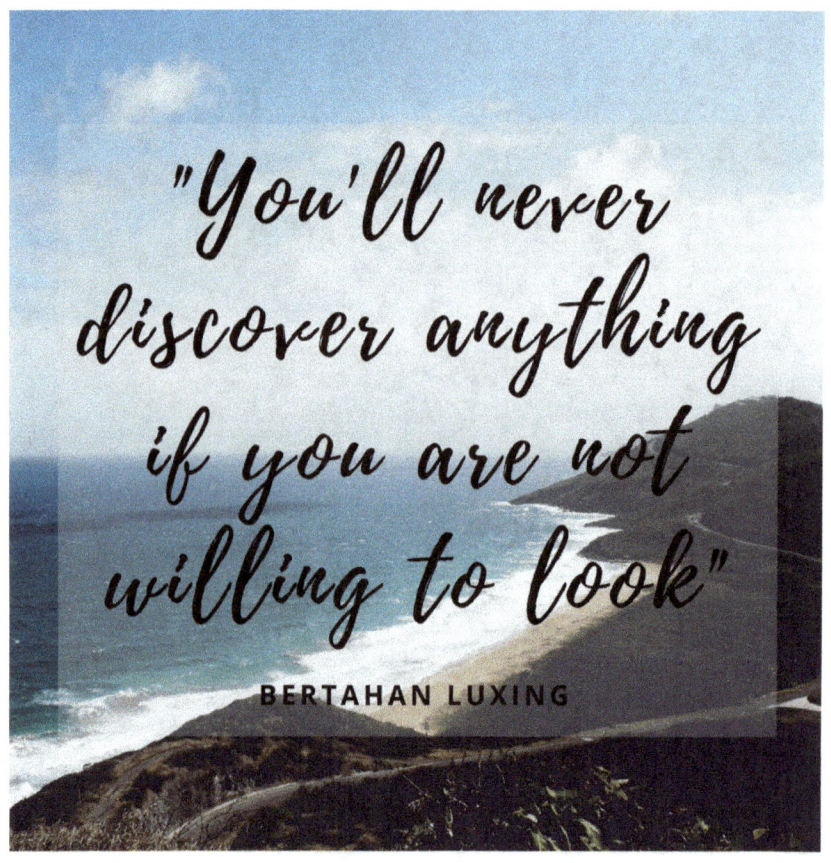

You'll never discover anything if you are not willing to look.

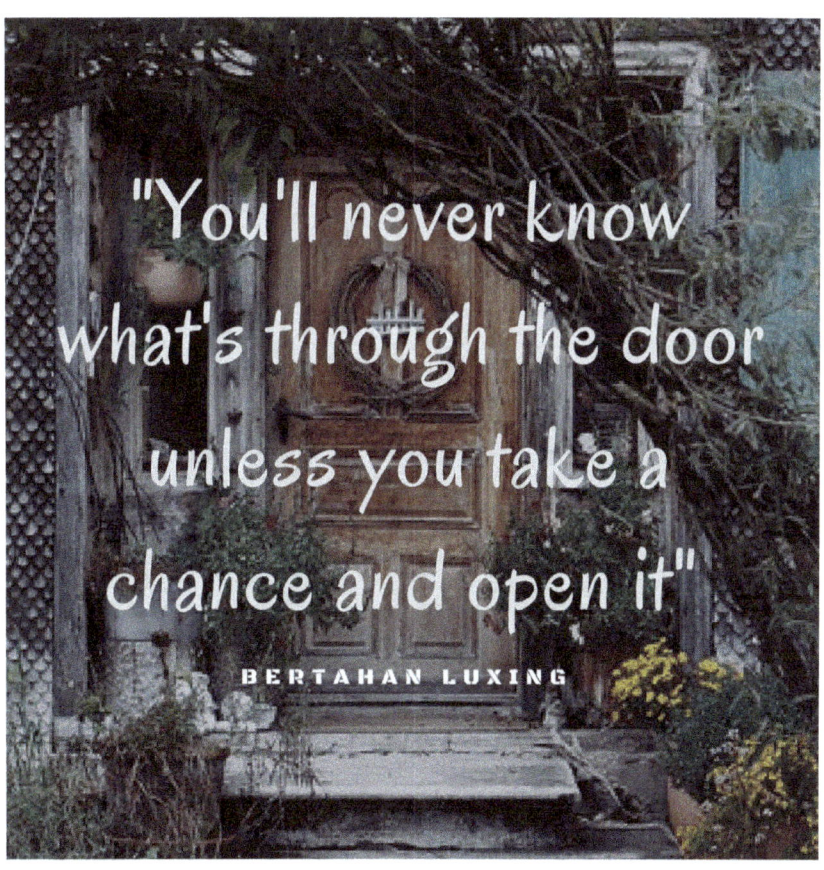

You'll never know what's through the door unless you take a chance and open it.

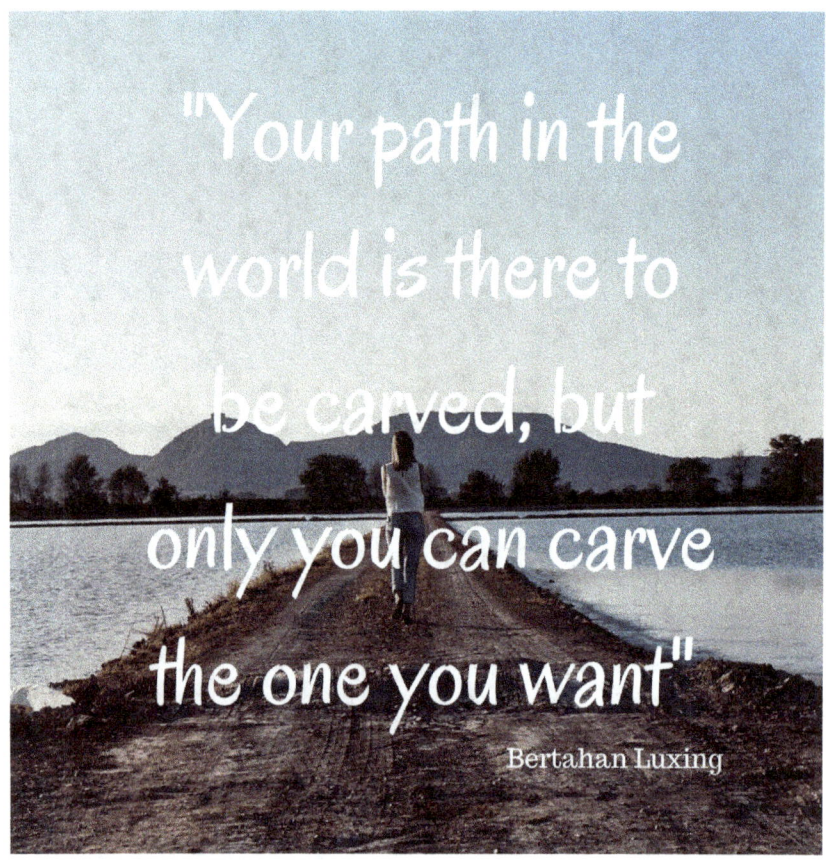

Your path in the world is there to be carved, but only you can carve the one you want.

Don't let fear hold you back.

Go experience the world.

I'd rather be content than rich.

It's only when they get lost that most people truly discover themselves.

It's time to get out of your bubble.

Just go out and see the world. Turn your dreams into memories.

Know what you want, get what you want, enjoy it. Don't forget step three. Many people do.

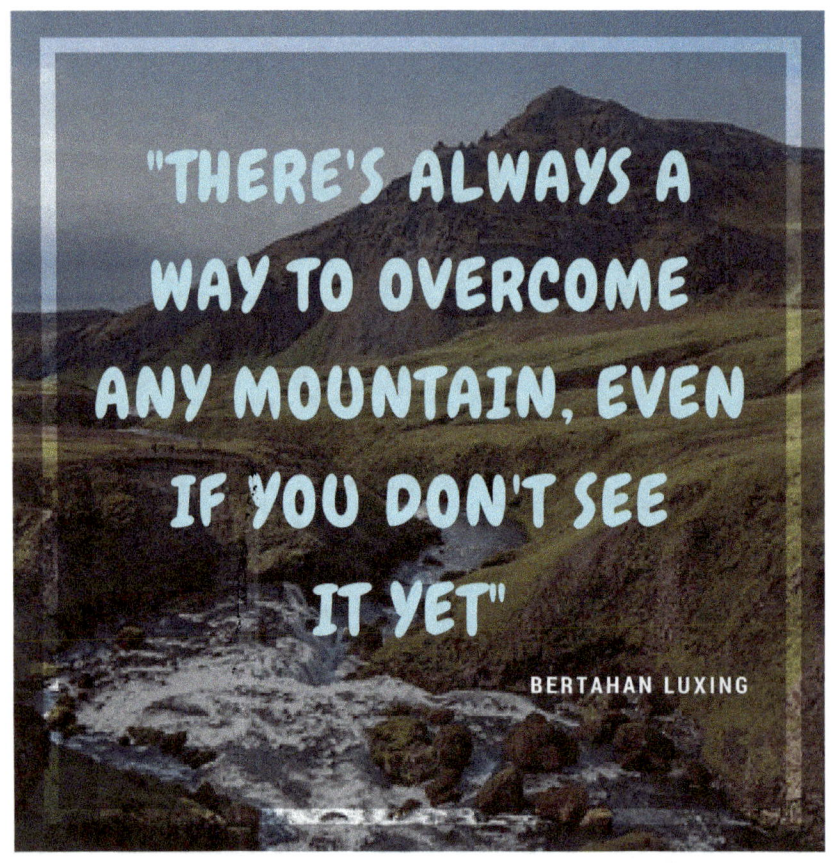

There's always a way to overcome any mountain, even if you don't see it yet.

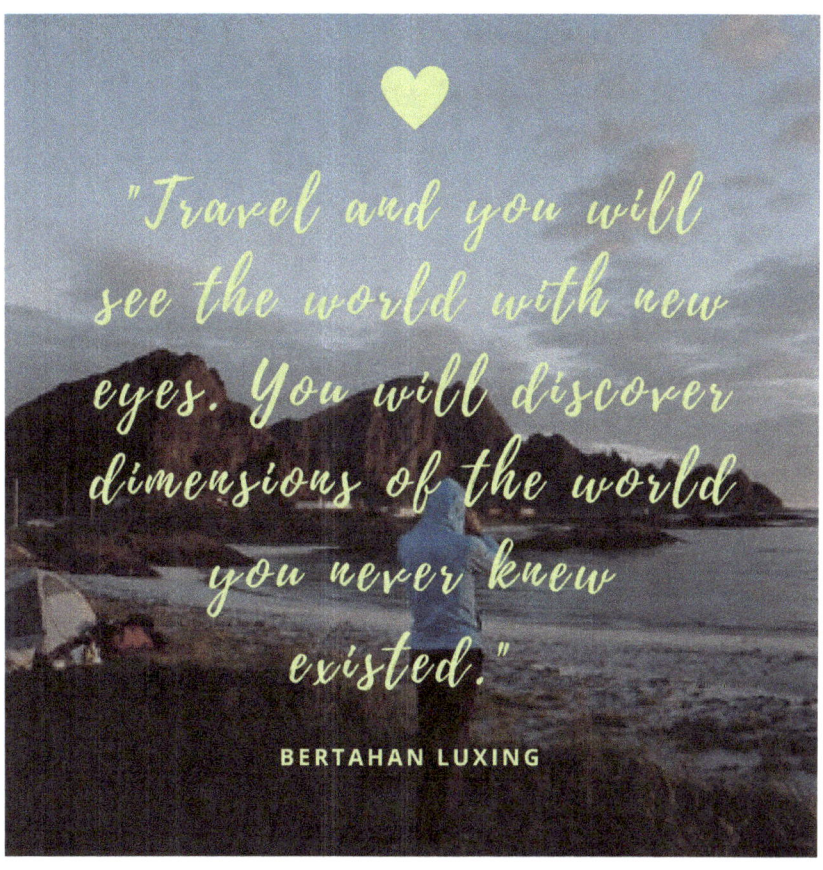

Travel and you will see the world with new eyes. You will discover dimensions of the world you never knew existed.

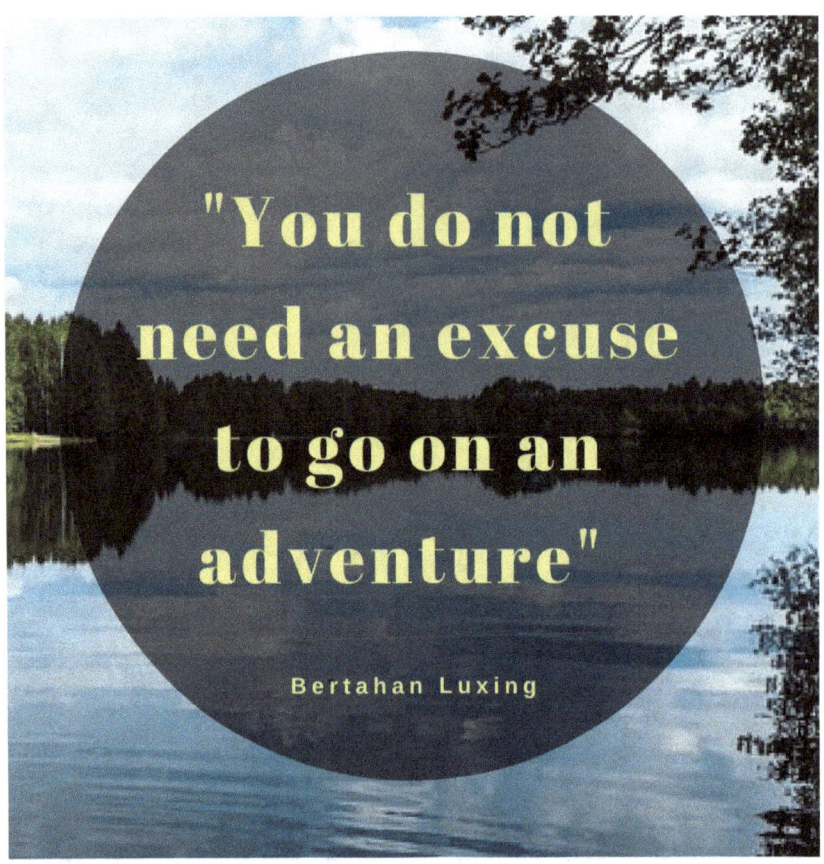

You do not need an excuse to go on an adventure.

Don't wait until the perfect time to go, the time may never be perfect.

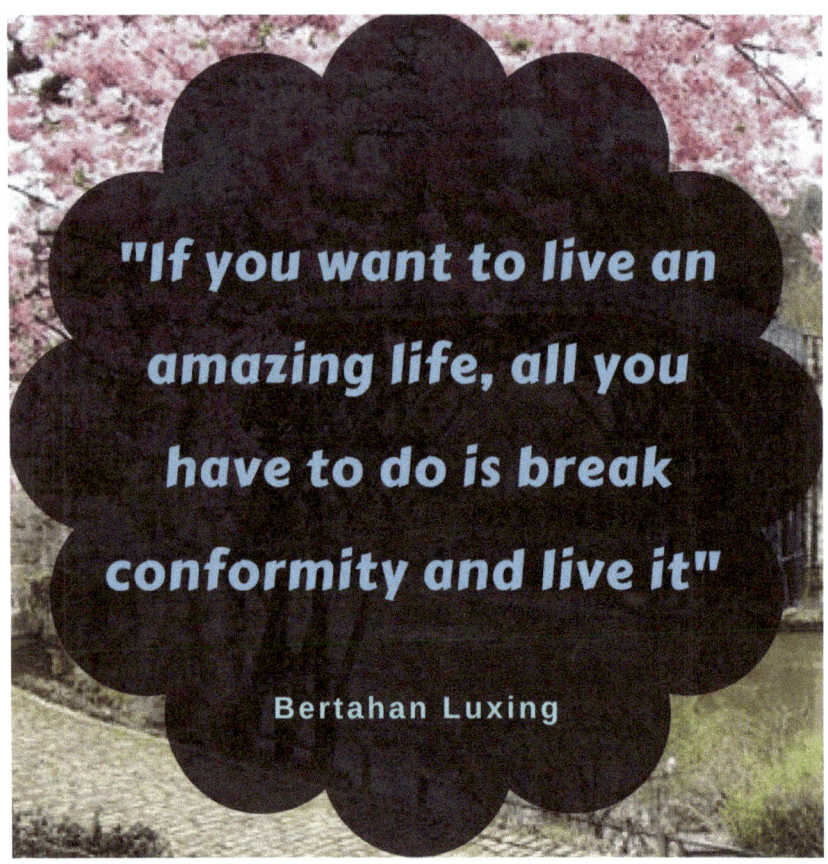

If you want to live an amazing life, all you have to do is break conformity and live it.

Make your reality whatever you want it to be.

No-one lives forever. Go experience as much as possible before you leave this place.

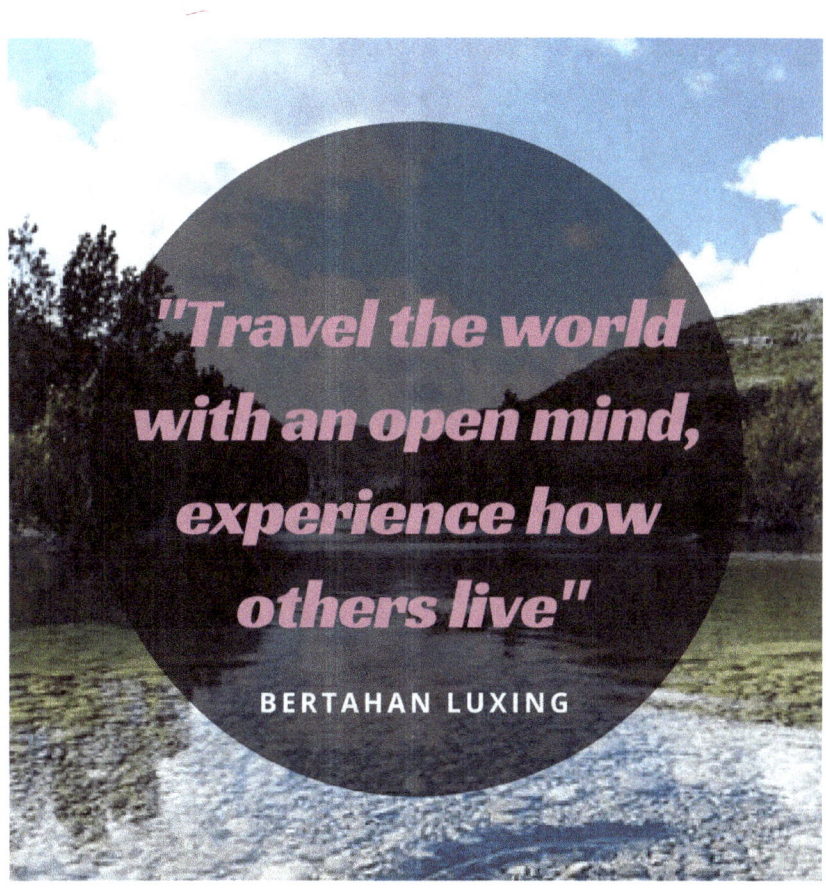

Travel the world with an open mind, experience how others live.

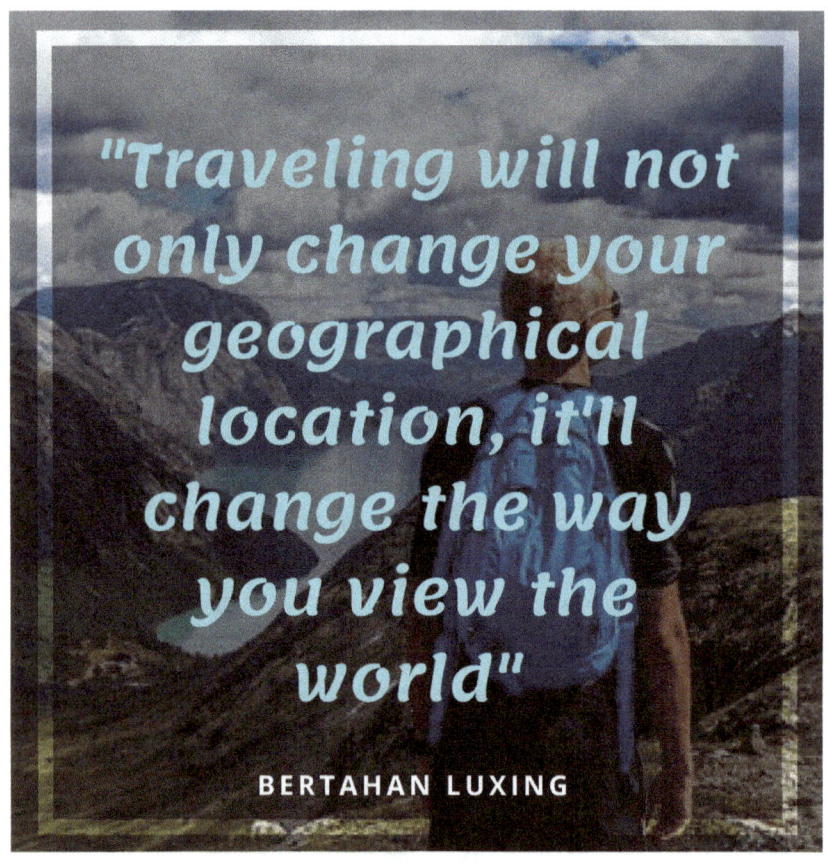

Traveling will not only change your geographical location, it'll change the way you view the world.

Usually the most magical places are not clearly marked on any map.

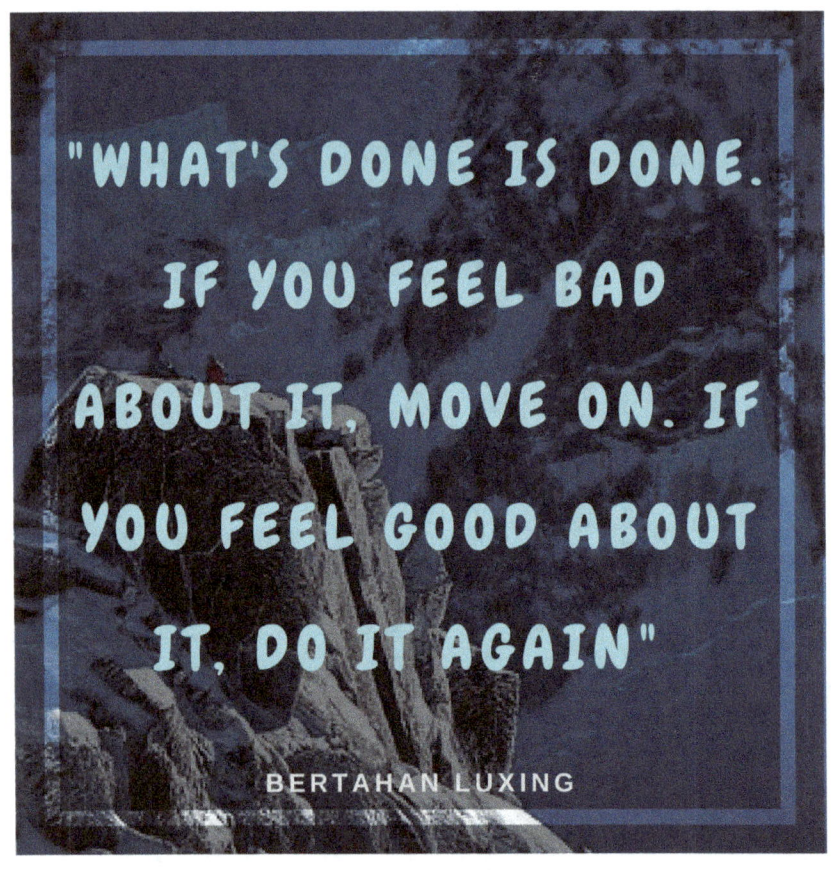

What's done is done. If you feel bad about it, move on. If you feel good about it, do it again.

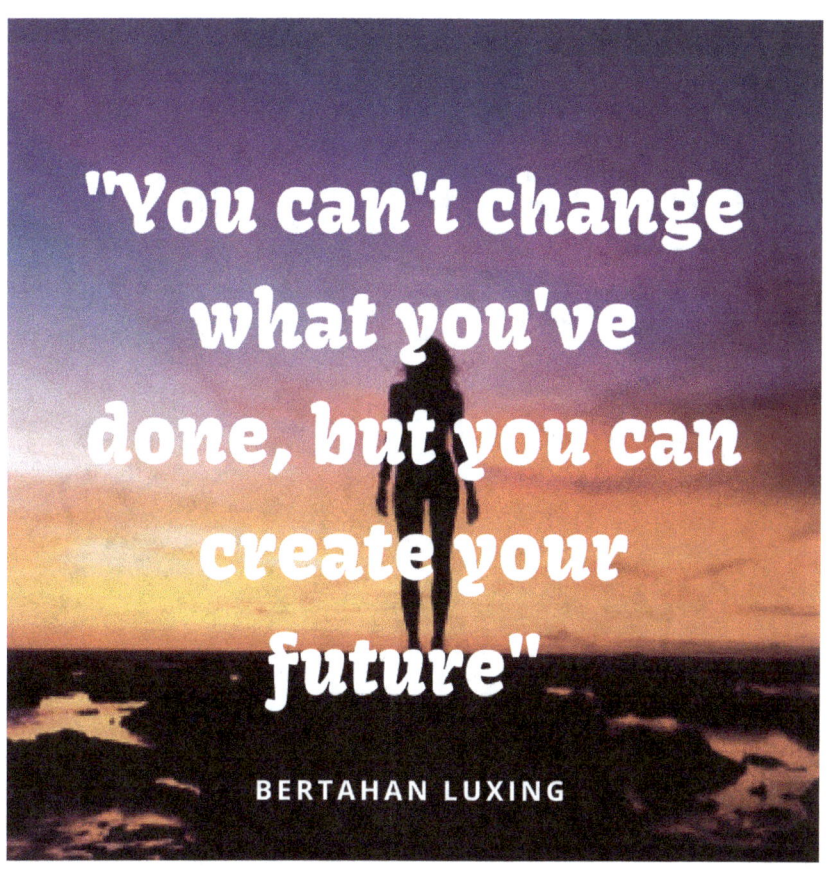

You can't change what you've done, but you can create your future.

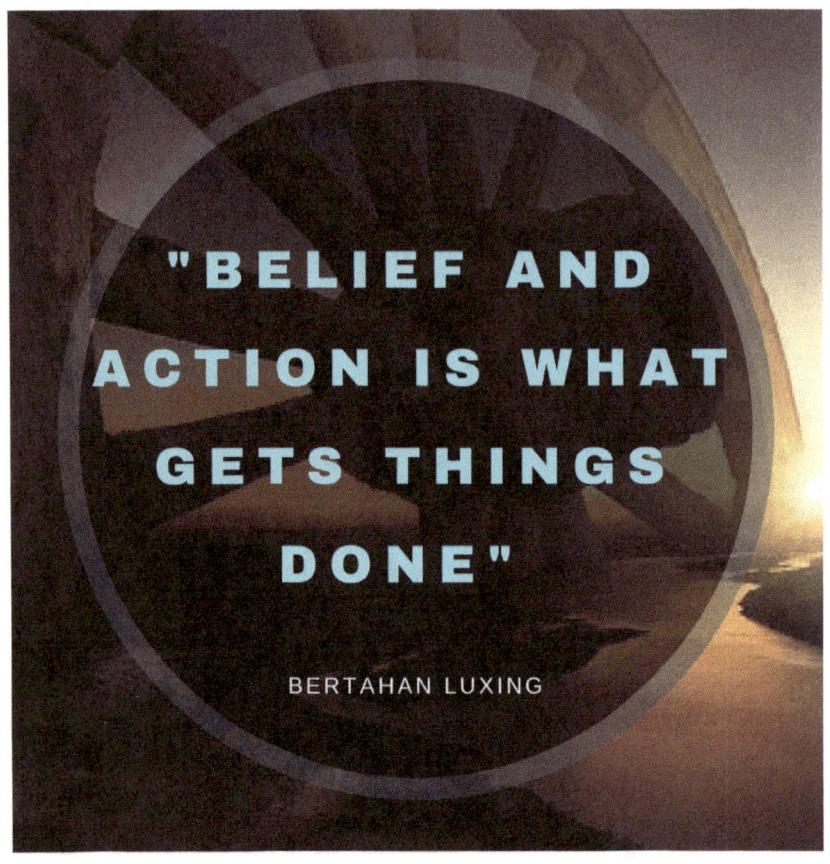

Belief and action is what gets things done.

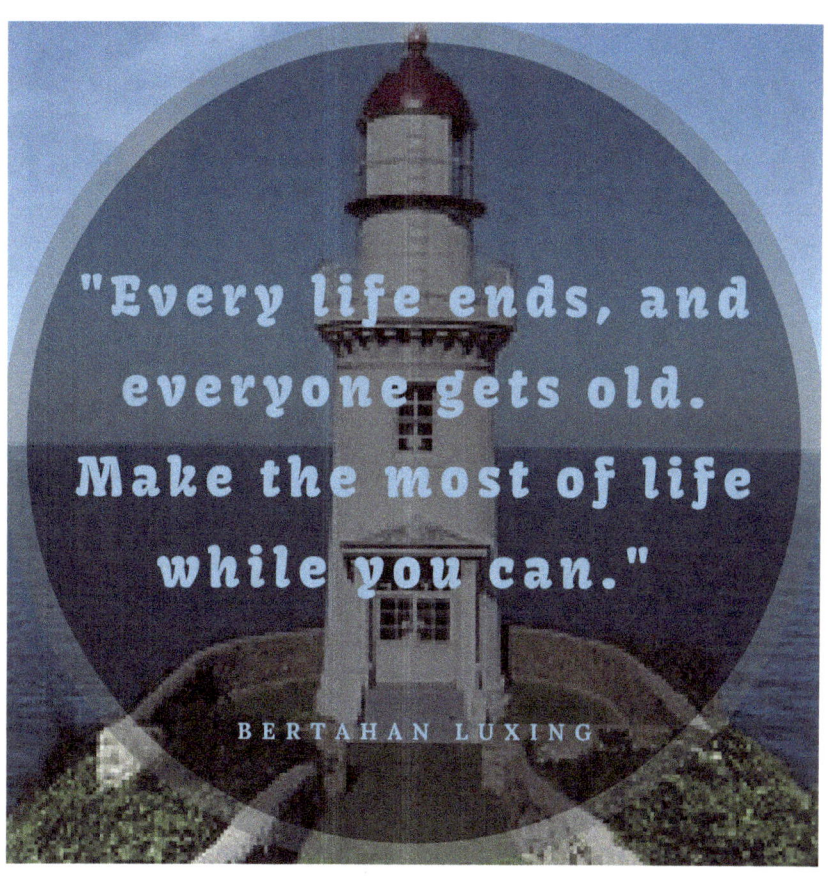

Every life ends, and everyone gets old. Make the most of life while you can.

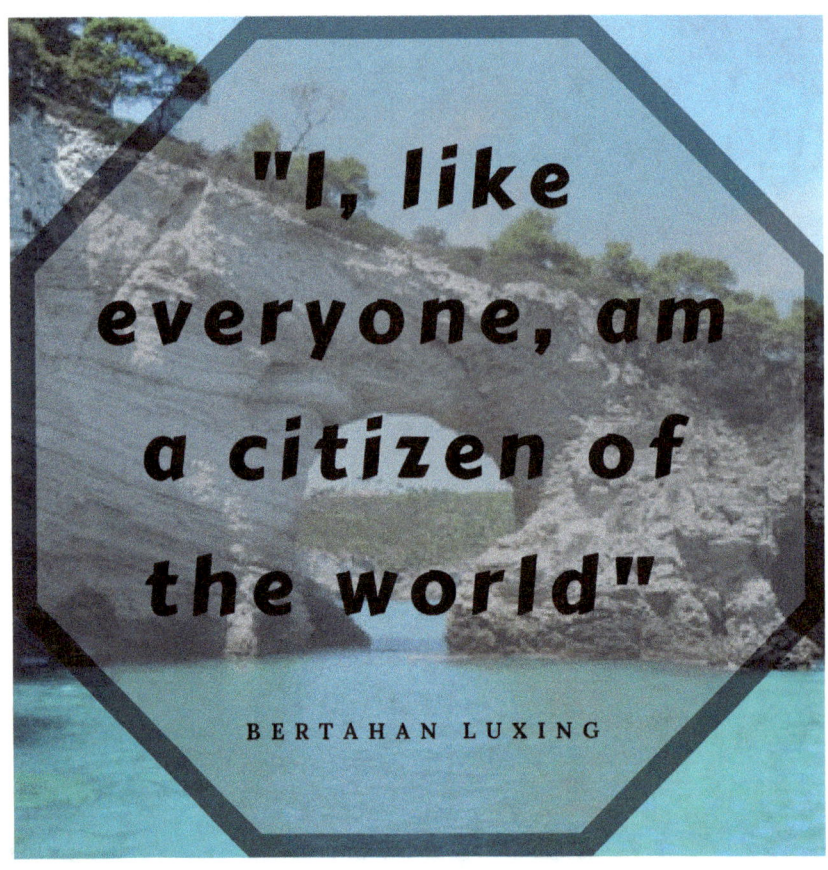

I, like everyone, am a citizen of the world.

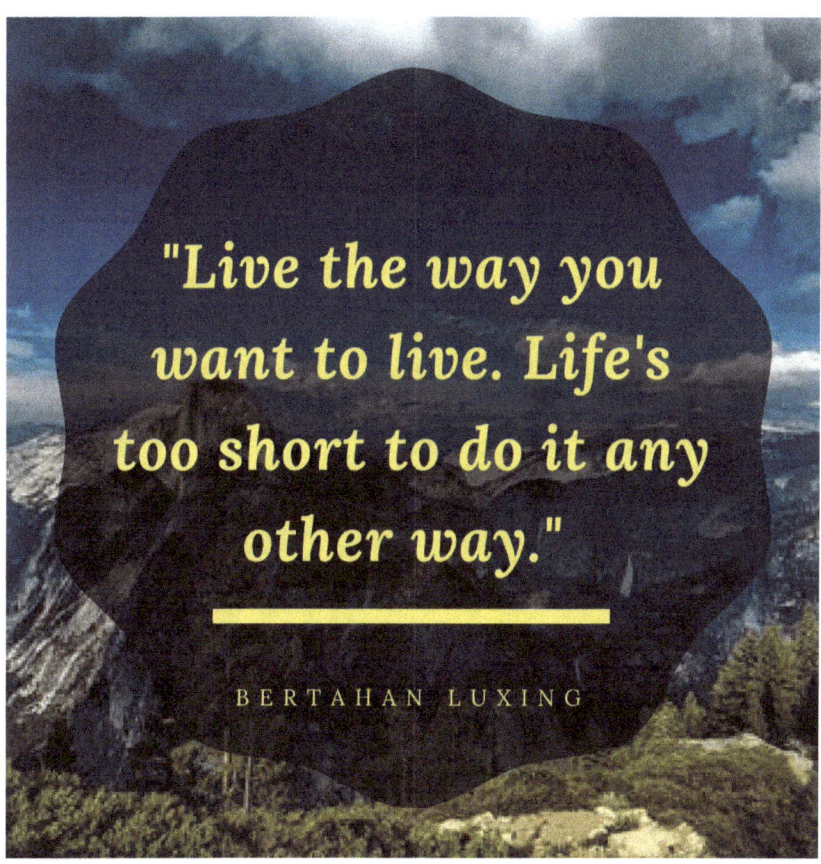

Live the way you want to live. Life's too short to do it any other way.

No matter where I travel to, I'm home.

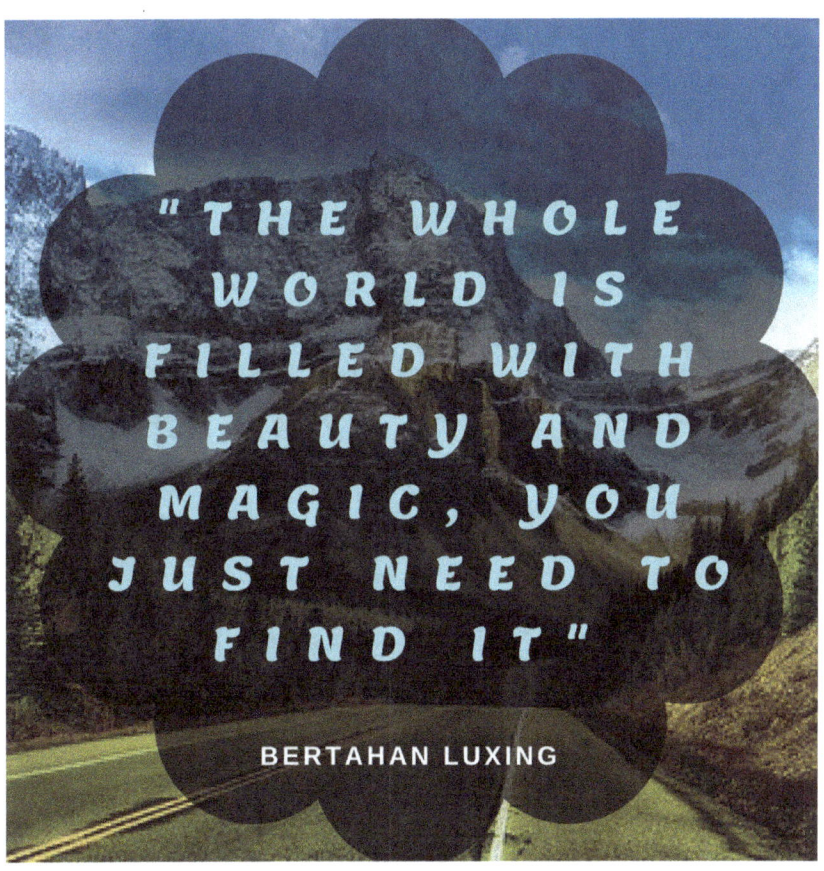

The whole world is filled with beauty and magic, you just need to find it.

Work towards living your daydream.

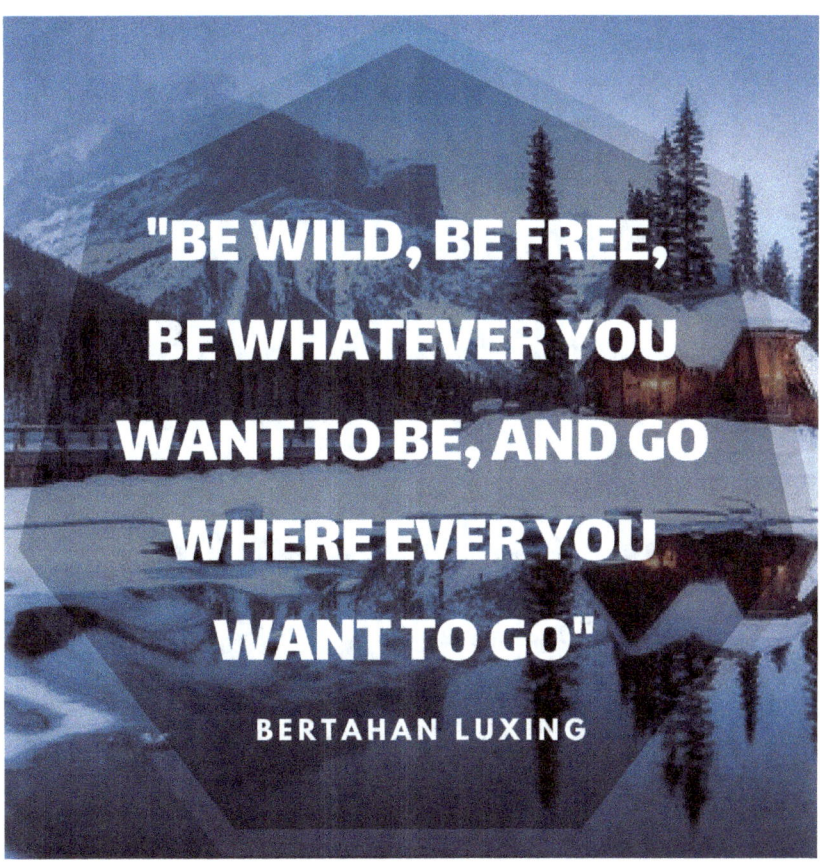

Be wild, be free, be whatever you want to be, and go where ever you want to go.

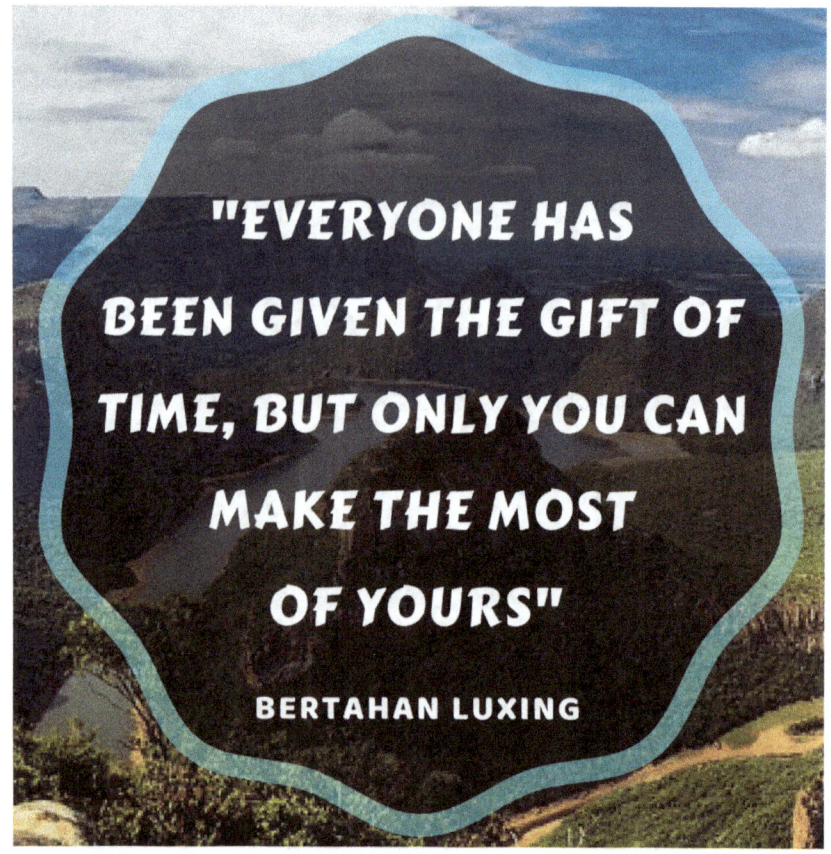

Everyone has been given the gift of time, but only you can make the most of yours.

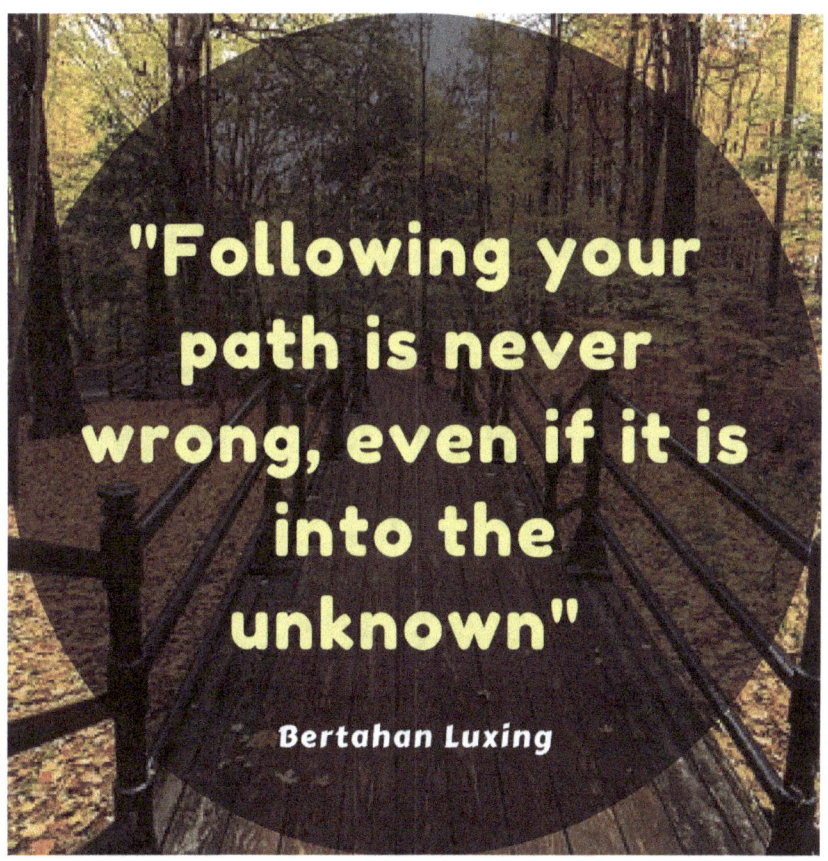

Following your path is never wrong, even if it is into the unknown.

Let's go get lost on an adventure.

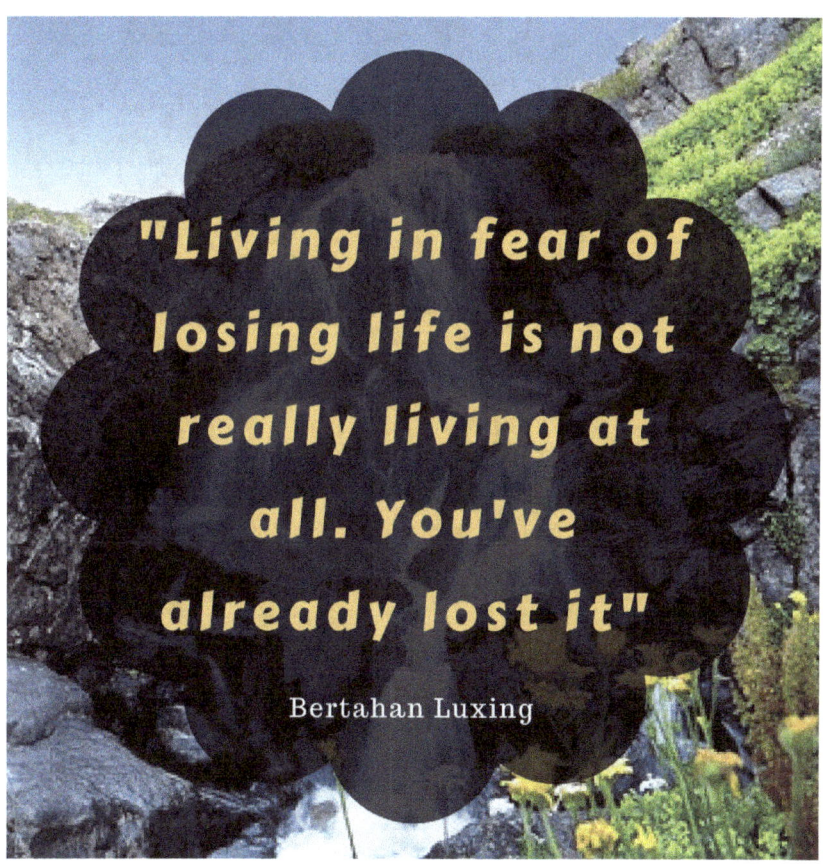

Living in fear of losing life is not really living at all. You've already lost it.

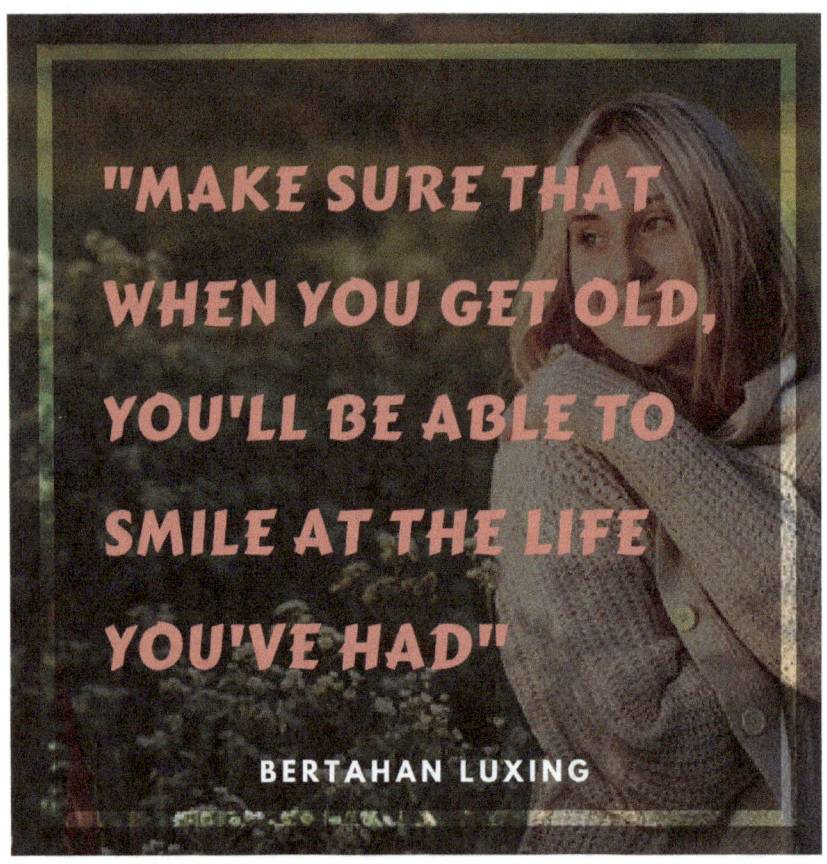

Make sure that when you get old, you'll be able to smile at the life you've had.

Make your life story a bestseller.

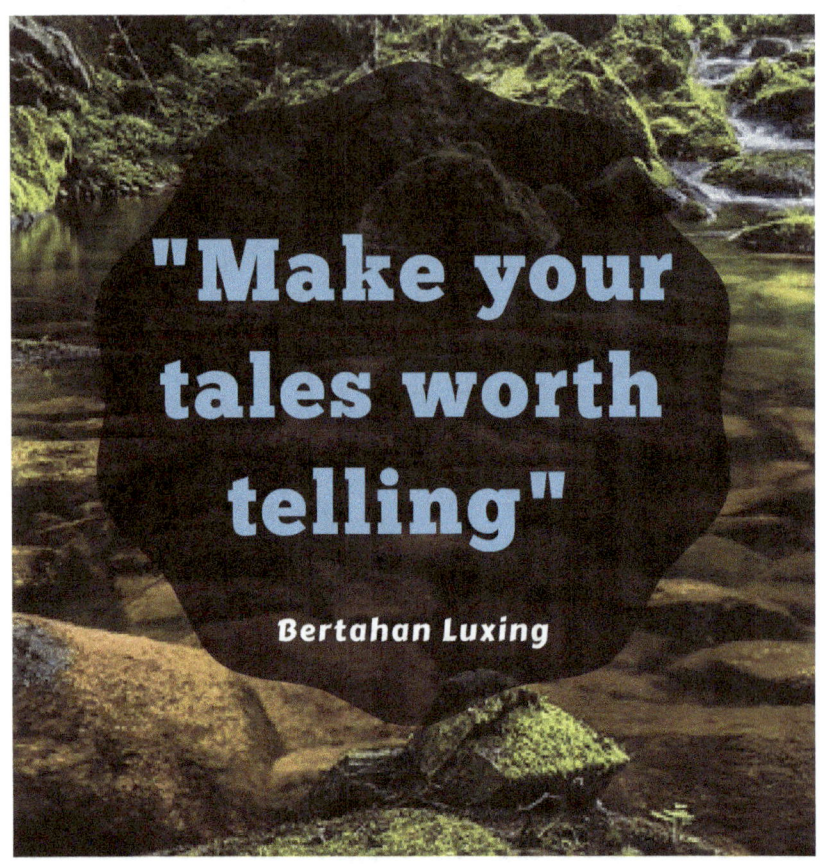

Make your tales worth telling.

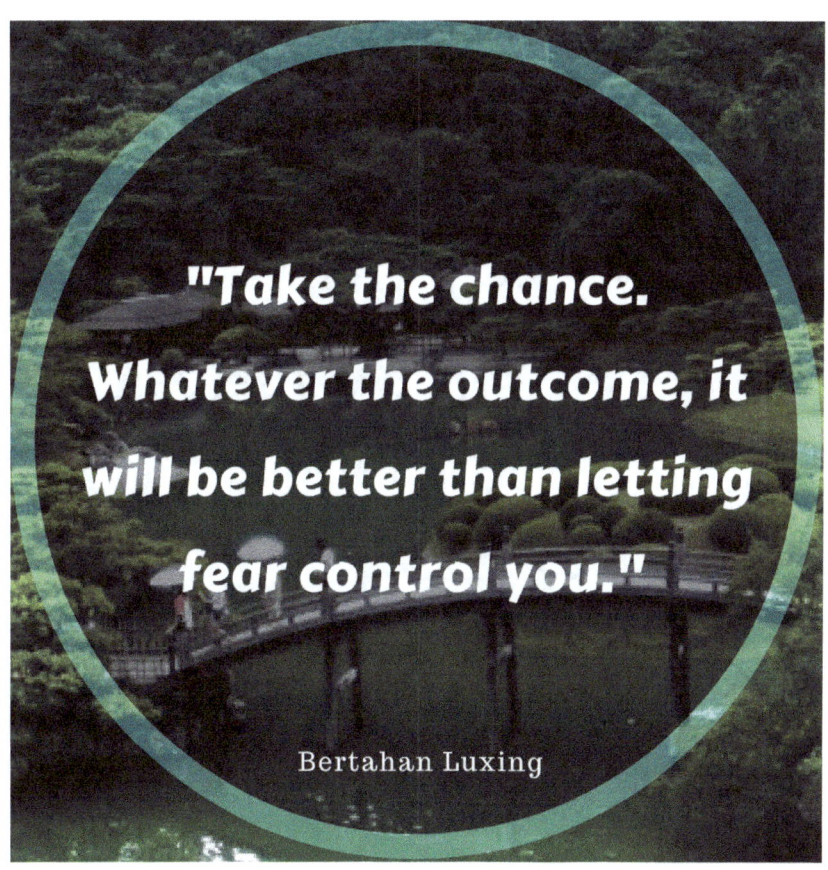

Take the chance. Whatever the outcome, it will be better than letter fear control you.

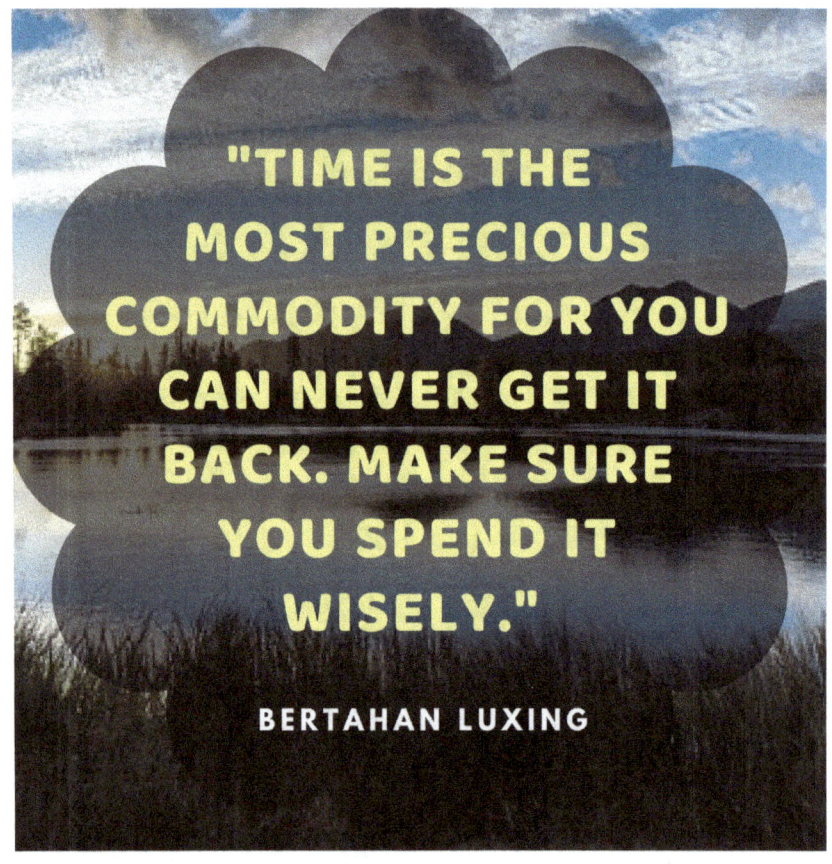

Time is the most precious commodity for you can never get it back. Make sure you spend it wisely.

Traveling light means shedding more than just physical baggage.

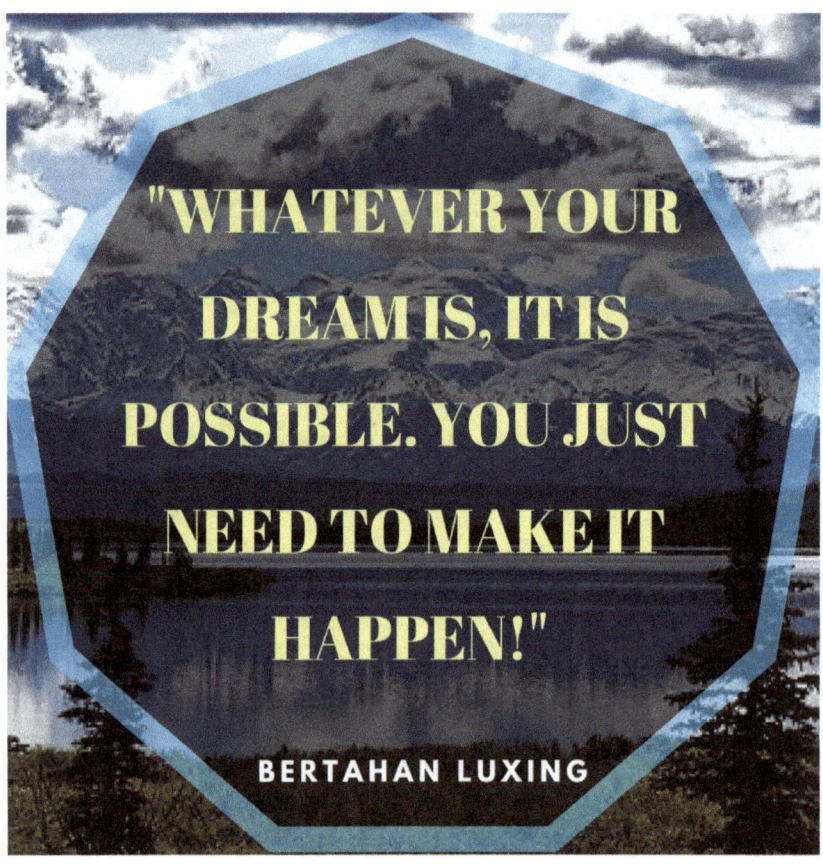

Whatever your dream is, it is possible. You just need to make it happen.

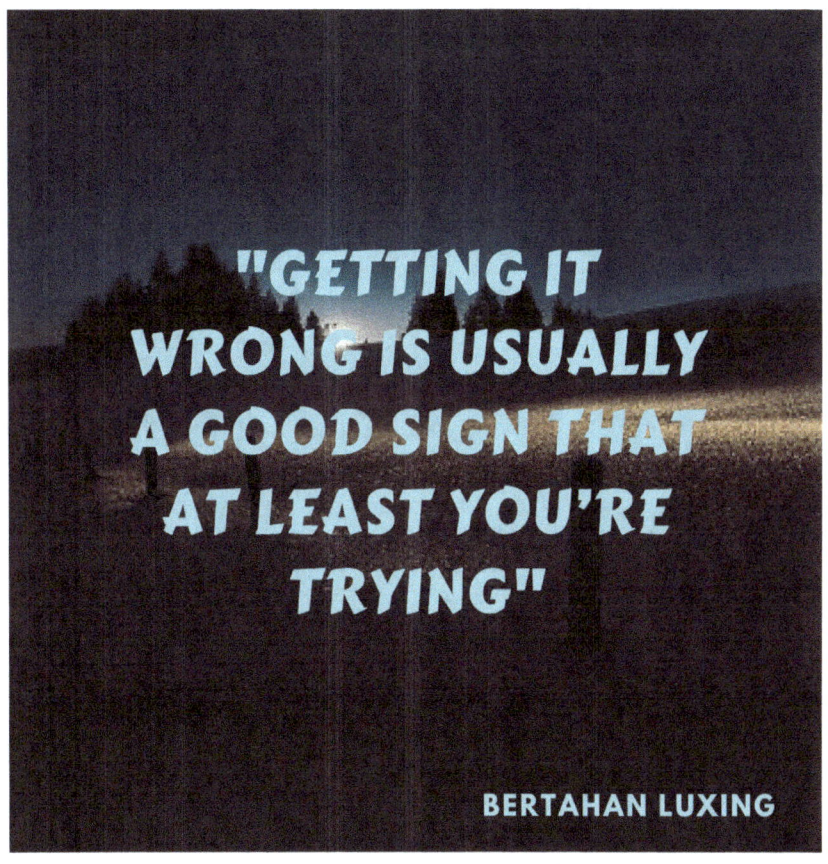

Getting it wrong is usually a good sign that at least you are trying.

Go discover the world for yourself.

I don't miss people. I remember them and smile.

> "I'd rather see something once in real life than watch it a million times on TV"
>
> Bertahan Luxing

I'd rather see something once in real life than watch it a million times on TV.

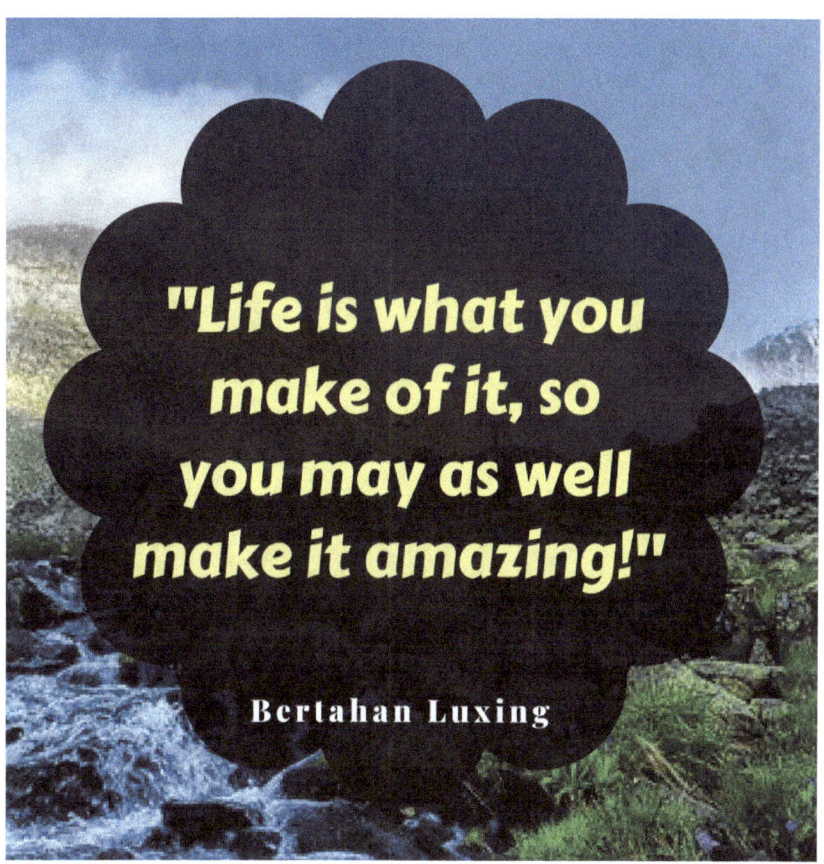

Life is what you make of it, so you may as well make it amazing.

Memories trump materials every time.

Merely existing is not living.

The less baggage you have, the lighter you will be, and the higher you can rise.

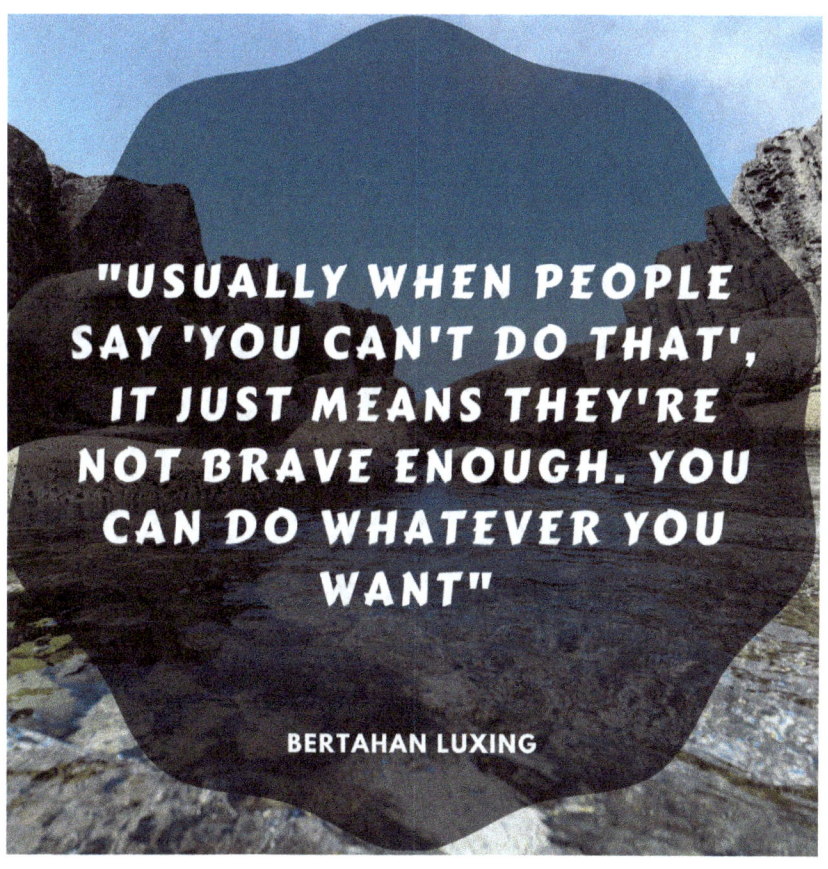

Usually when people say 'you can't do that', it just means they're not brave enough. You can do whatever you want.

Work towards maximizing time, not materials.

Doing the same thing every day is not really living.

Even just moving slowly towards your dreams is faster than most people.

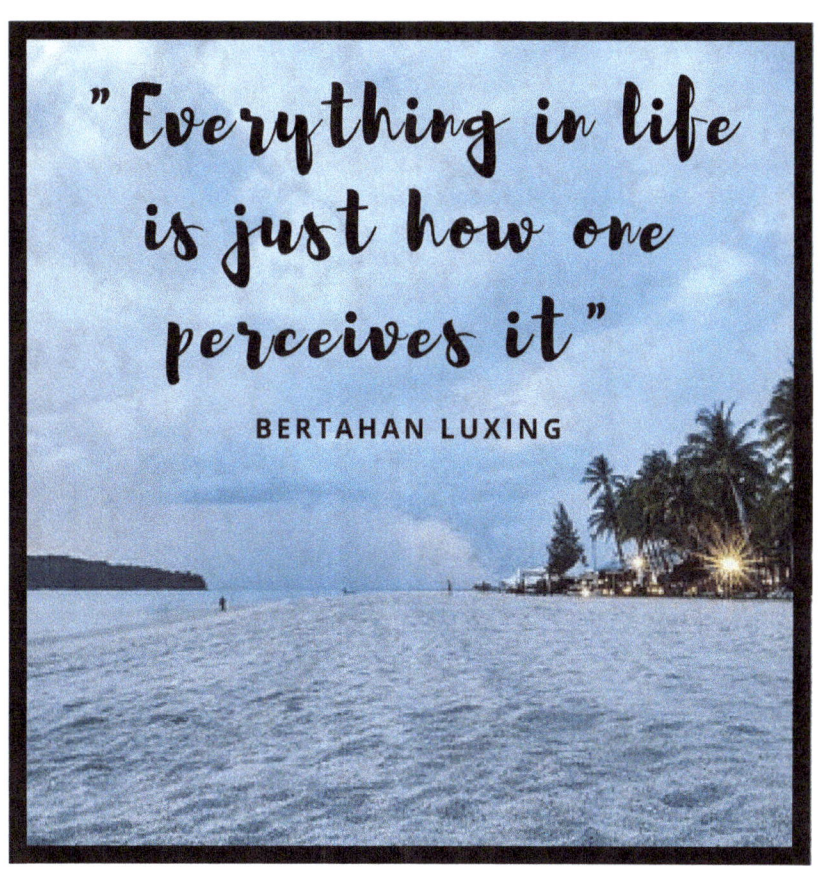

Everything in life is just how one perceives it.

Experiences, not things.

Go on, get lost.

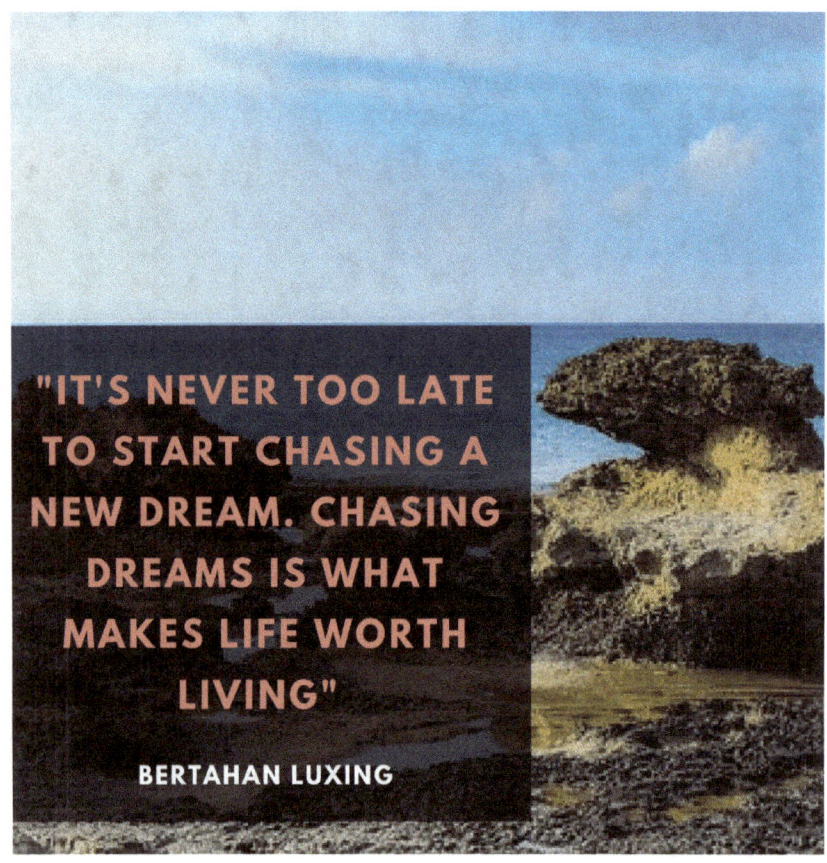

It's never too late to start chasing a new dream. Chasing dreams is what makes life worth living.

Live the adventure that is life.

Only you can create the life you dream of.

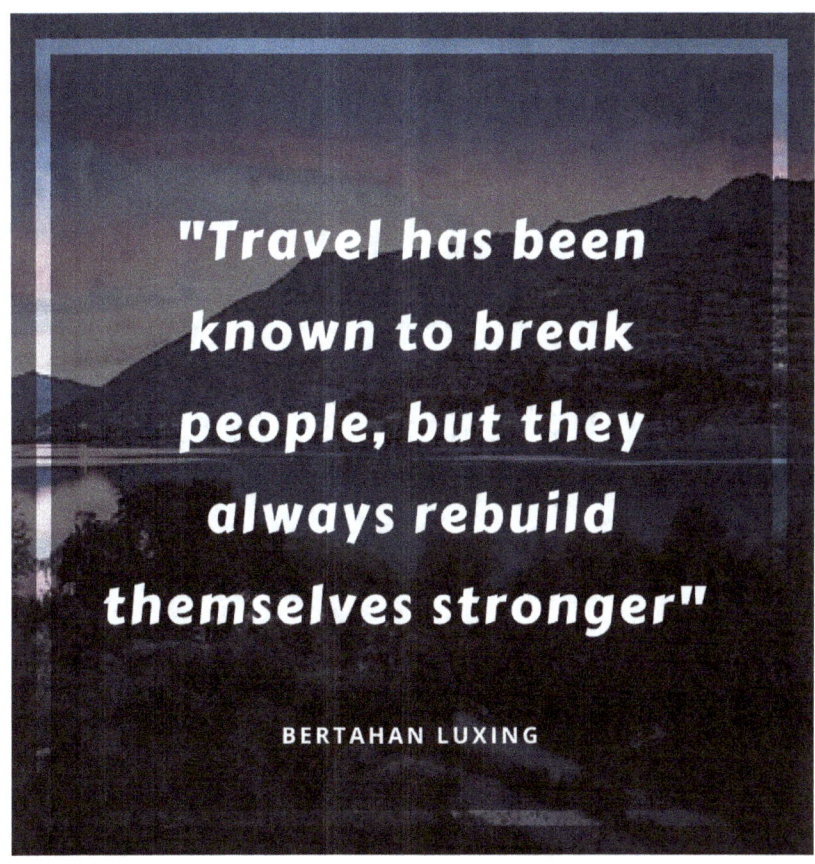

Travel has been known to break people, but they always rebuild themselves stronger.

Traveling may be the fastest way to discover and/or create yourself.

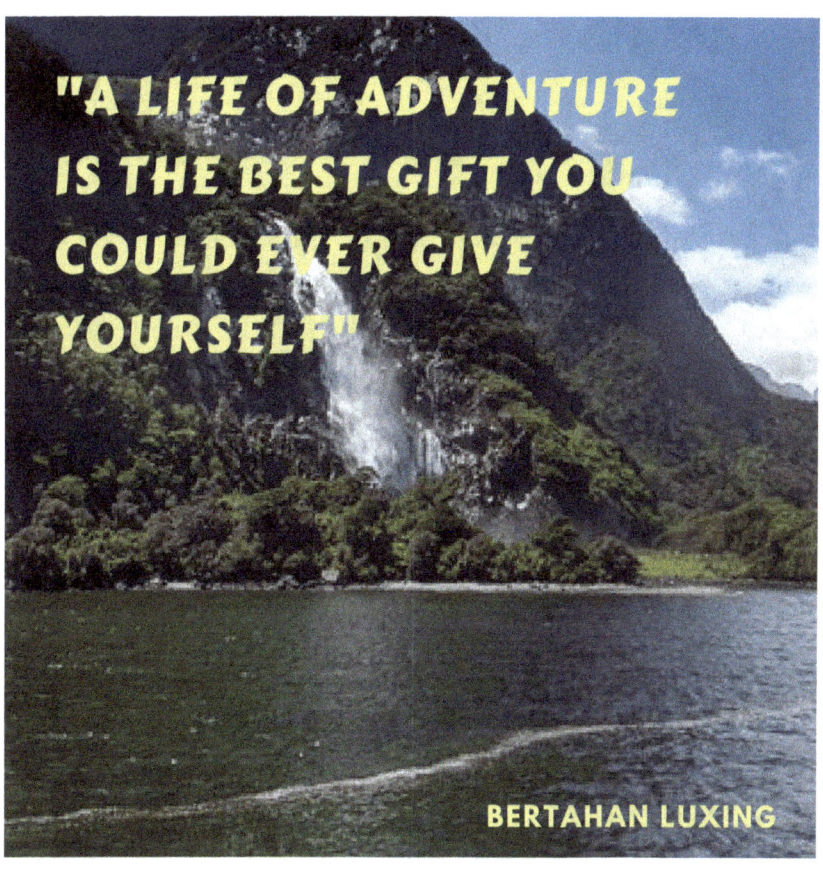

A life of adventure is the best gift you could ever give yourself.

Be brave in this, your experiment of life.

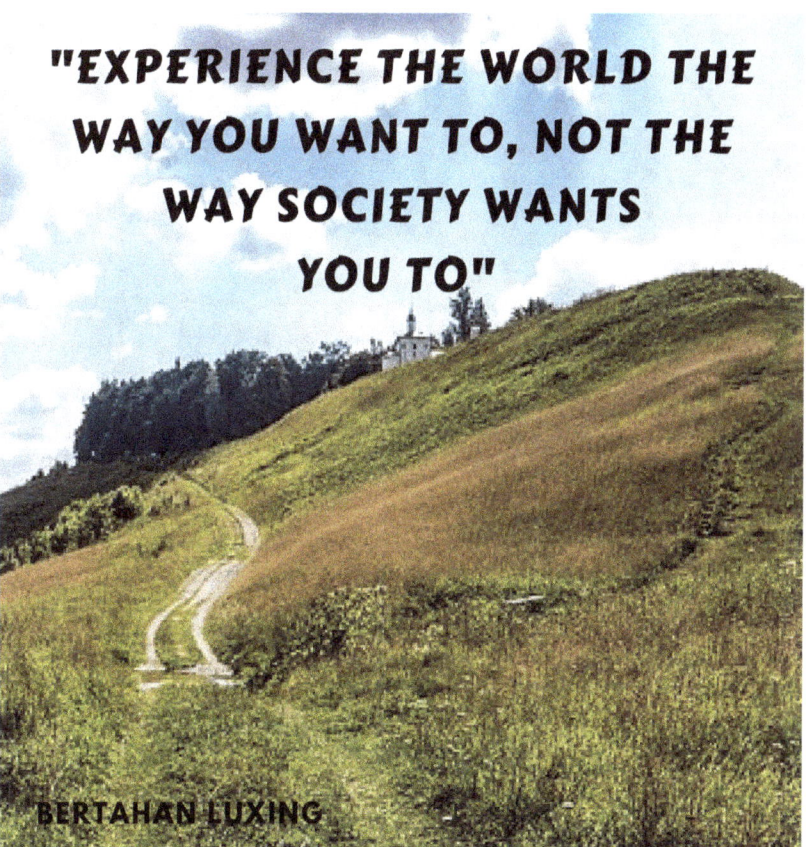

Experience the world the way you want to, not the way society wants you to.

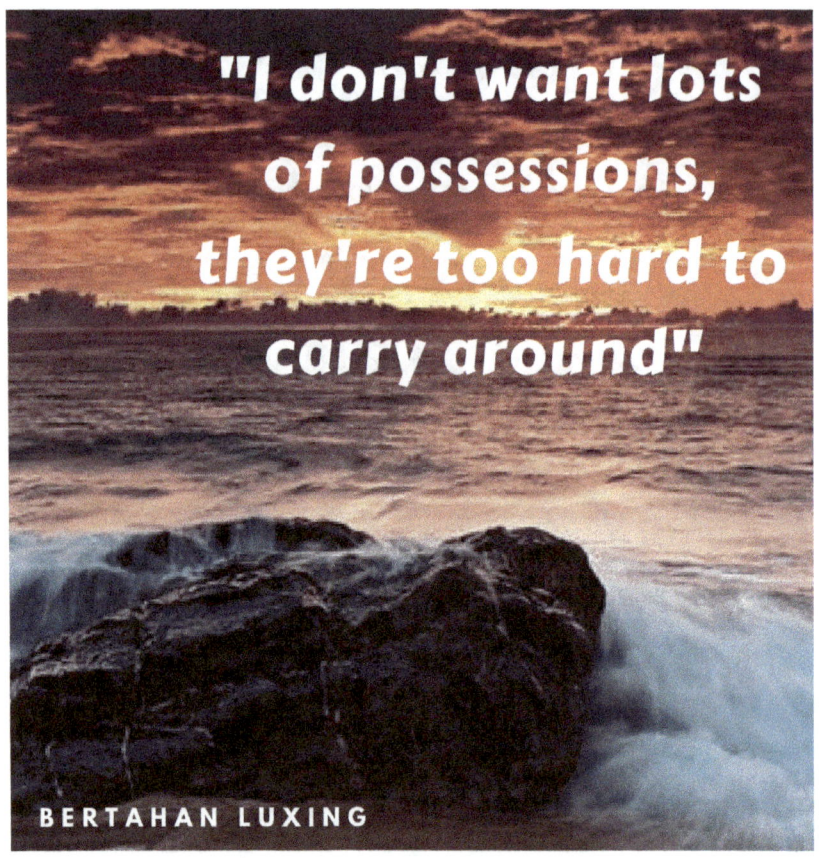

I don't want lots of possessions, they're too hard to carry around.

I'd rather travel like a bum than be a slave to society.

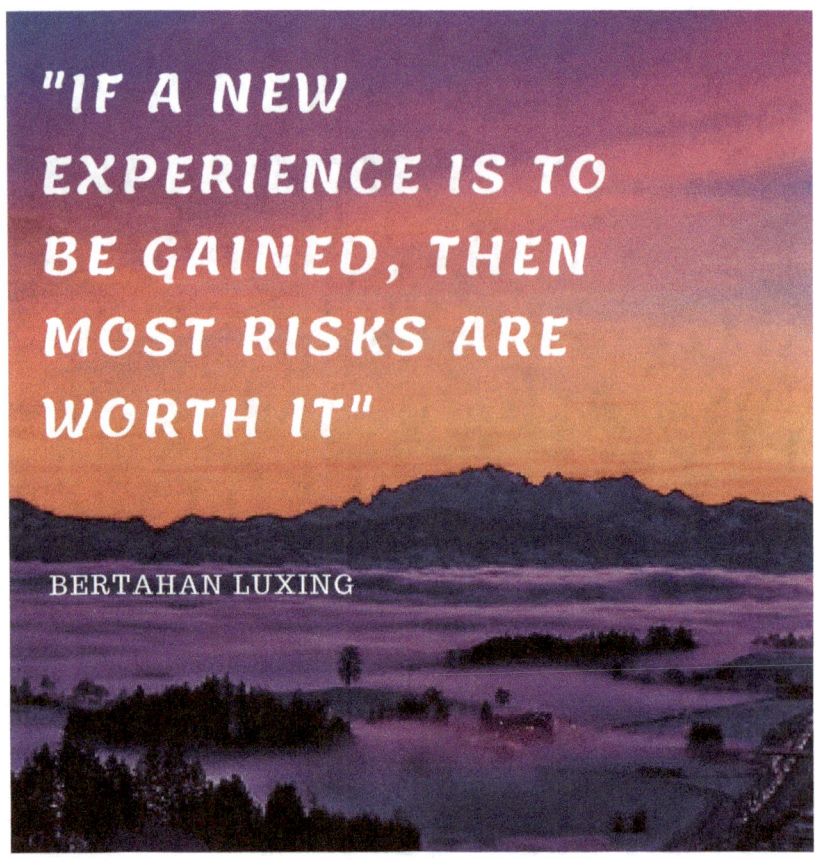

If a new experience is to be gained, then most risks are worth it.

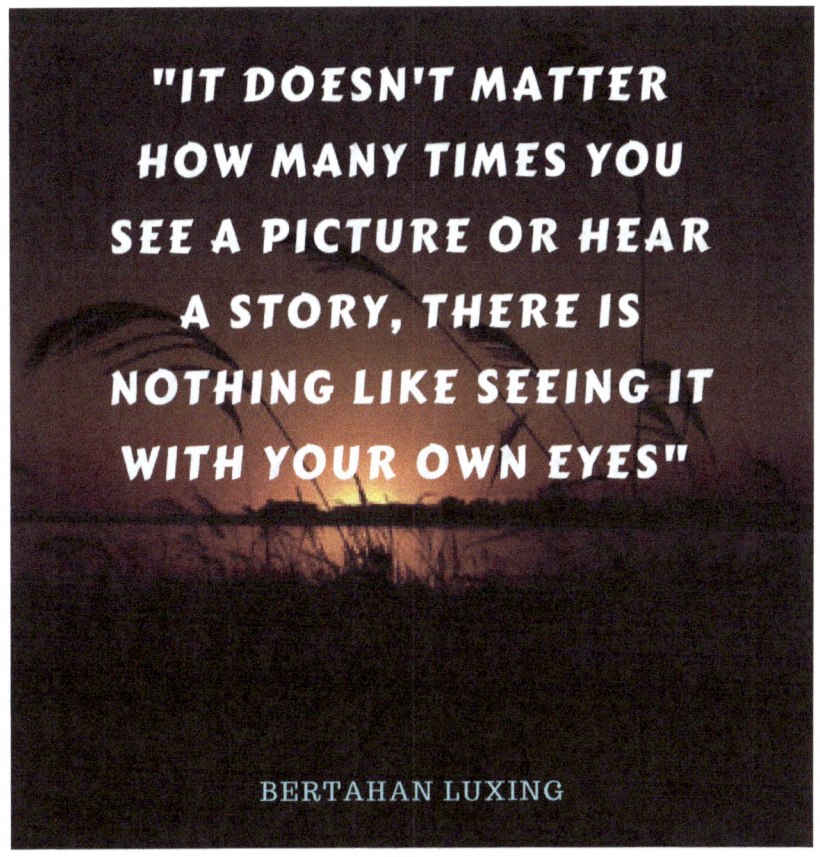

It doesn't matter how many times you see a picture or hear a story, there is nothing like seeing it with your own eyes.

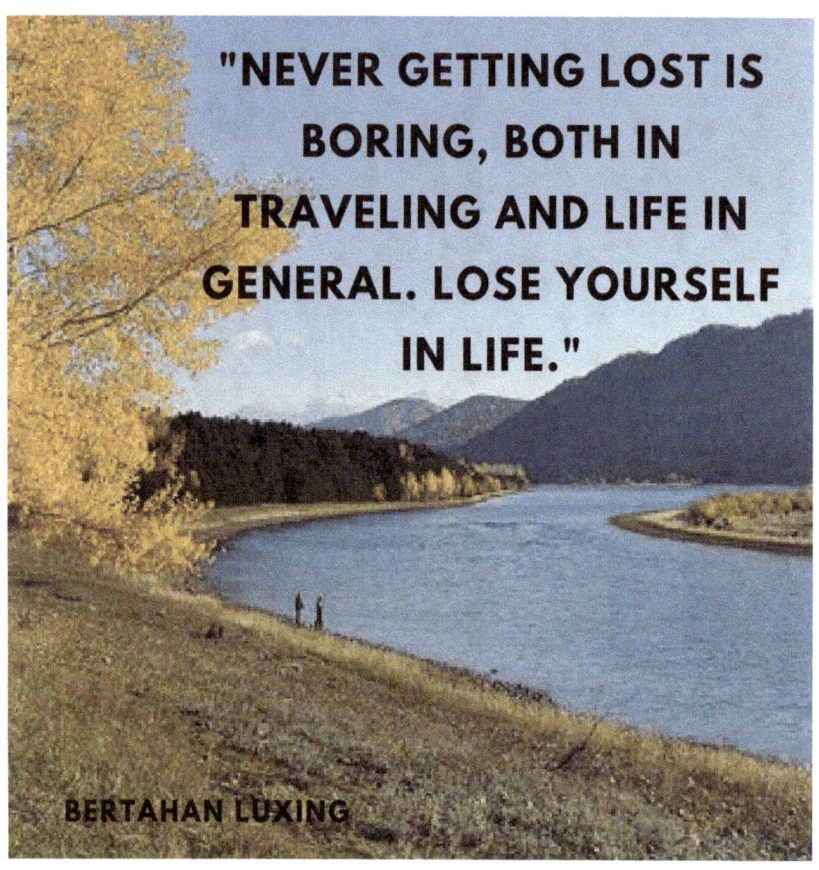

*Never getting lost is boring, both in traveling and life in general.
Lose yourself in life.*

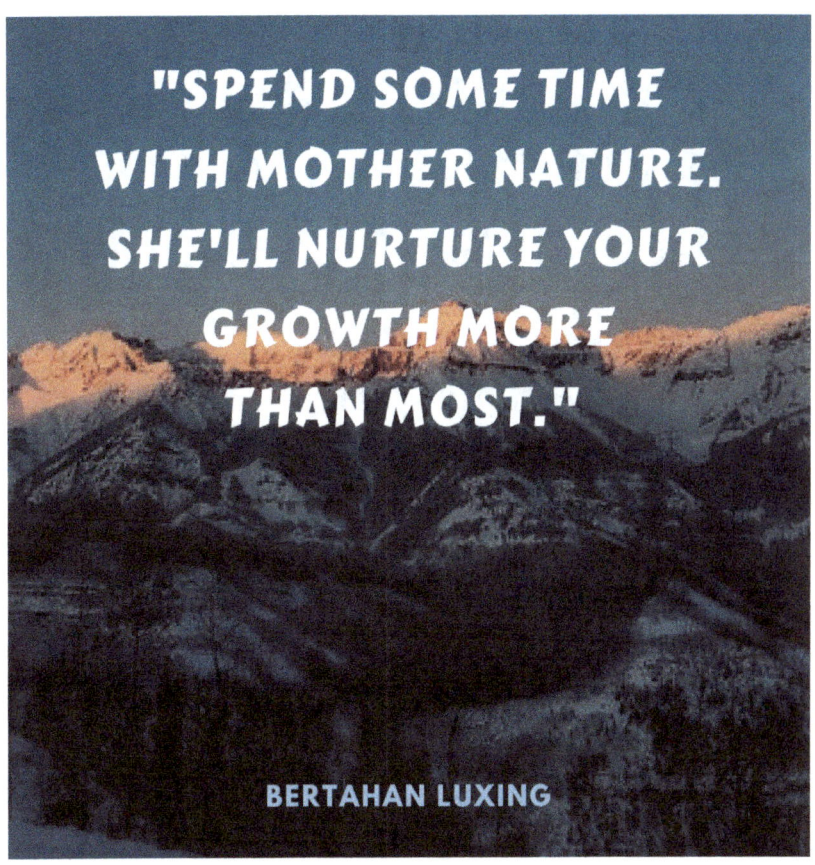

Spend some time with mother nature. She'll nurture your growth more than most.

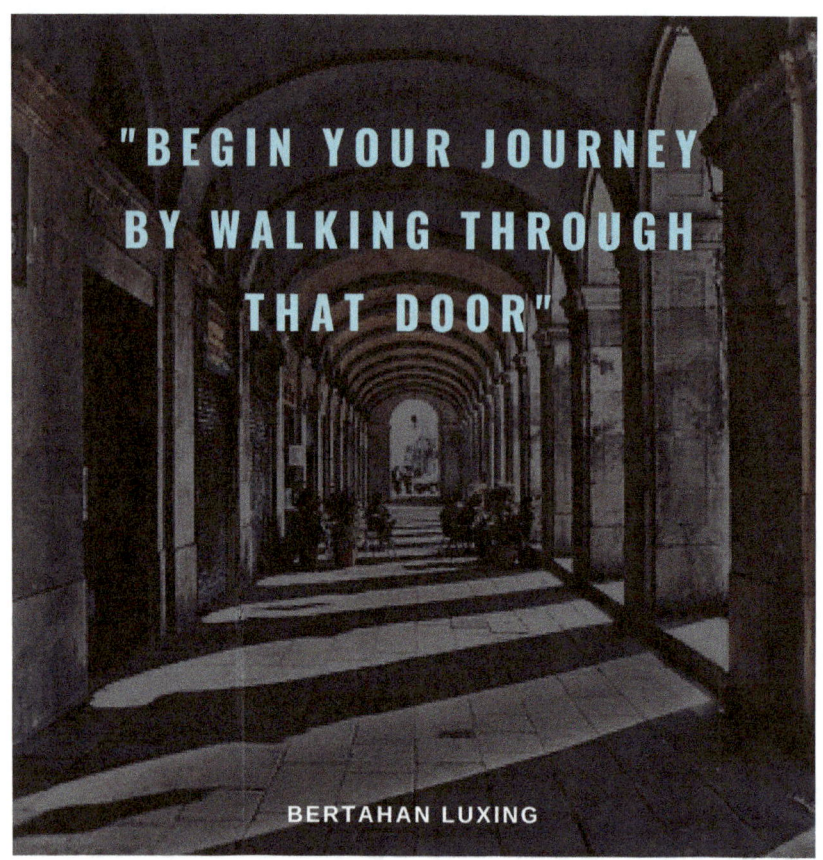

Begin your journey by walking through that door.

Don't let others write your life story. Hold your own pen.

Dull routine is deadlier than any adventure.

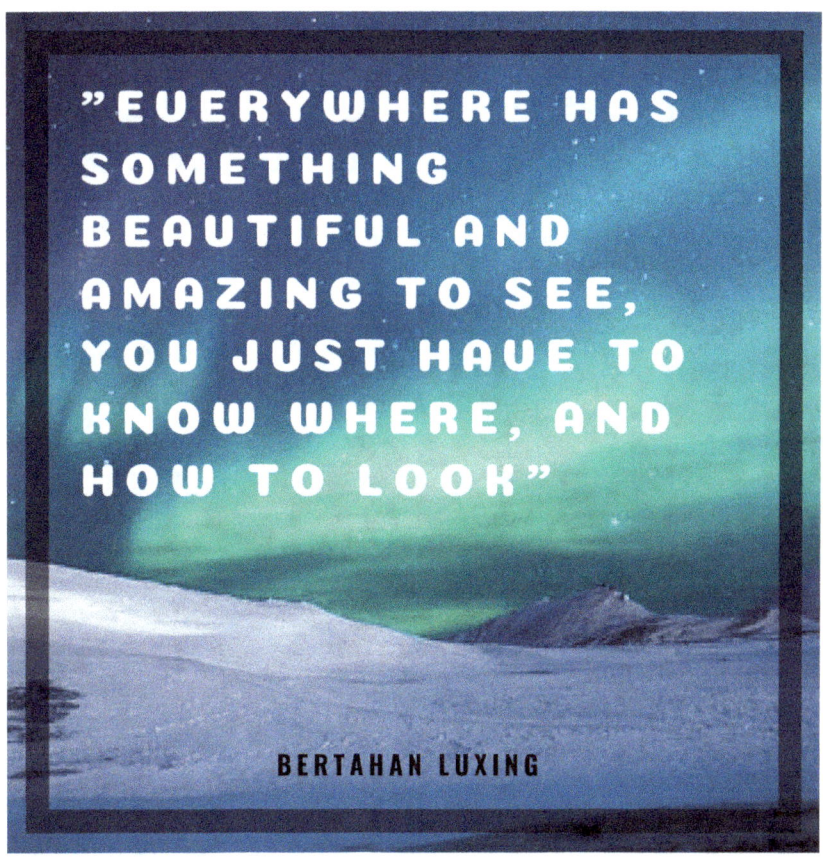

Everywhere has something beautiful and amazing to see, you just have to know where, and how to look.

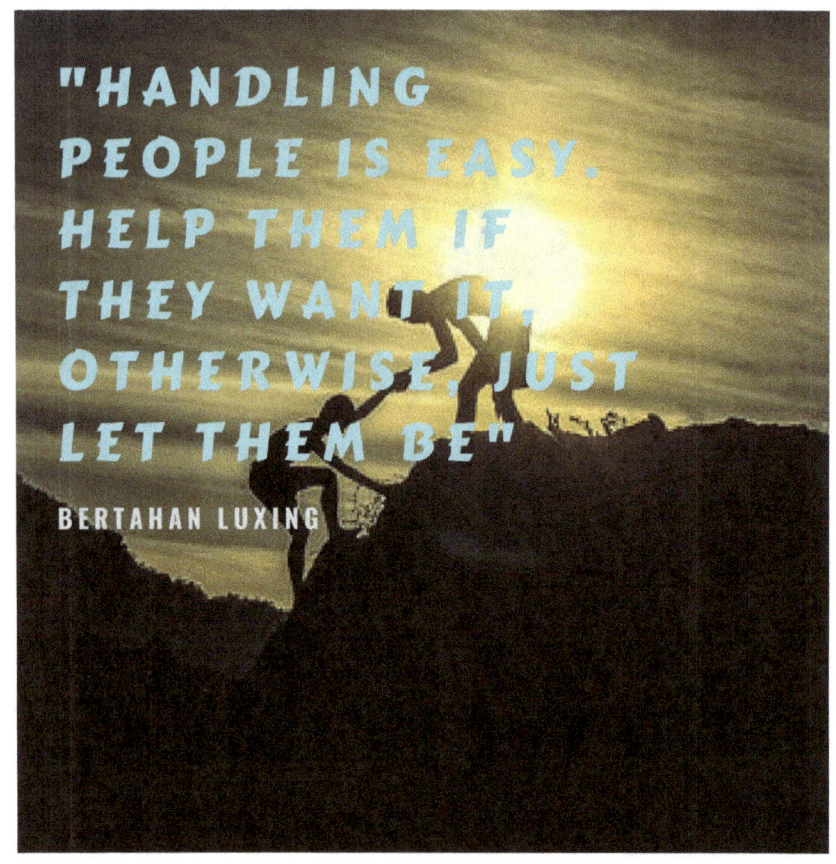

Handling people is easy. Help them is they want it, otherwise, just let them be.

Keep exploring, there's something new to discover around every corner.

Let the journey take you.

Life is meant to be enjoyed.

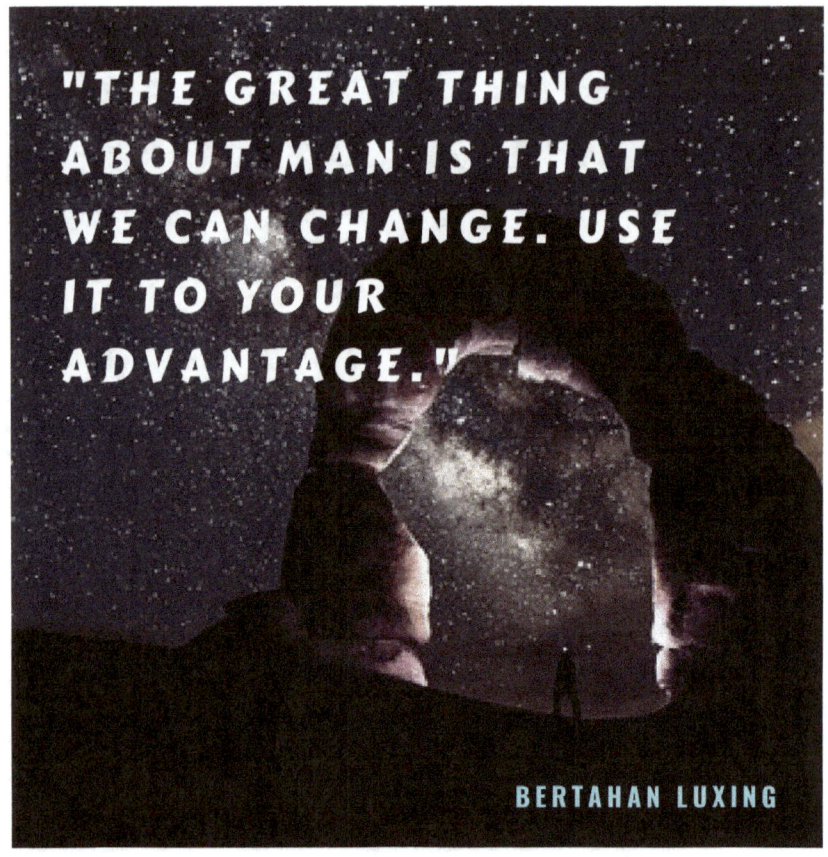

The great thing about man is that we can change. Use it to your advantage.

The world is my home.

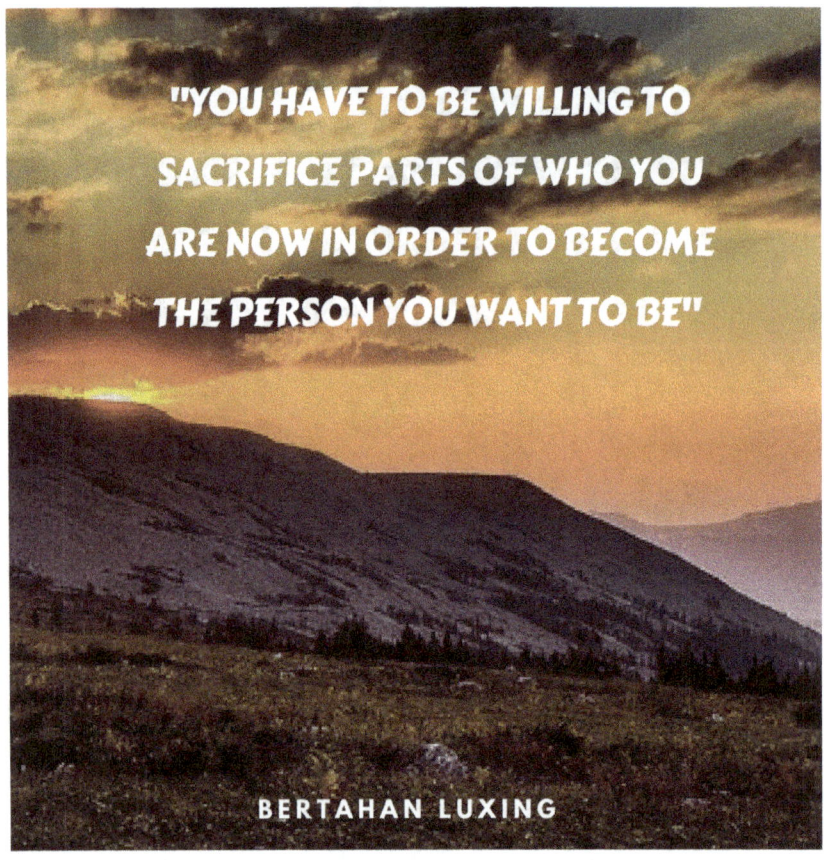

You have to be willing to sacrifice parts of who are now in order to become the person you want to be.

Don't let a moment of fear cause you a lifetime of regret.

If you can imagine you are free, then you are.

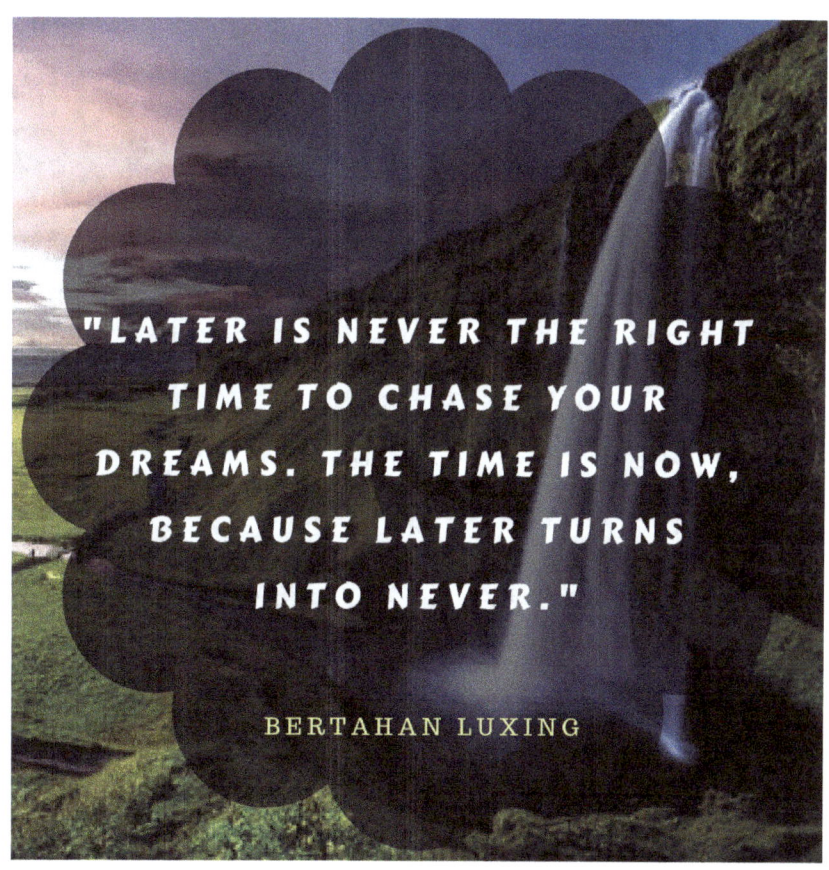

Later is never the right time to chase your dreams. The time is now, because later turns into never.

Look around, the whole world is a playground.

Making plans is good, but don't wait until the 'perfect' time to act upon them, because the perfect time may never come.

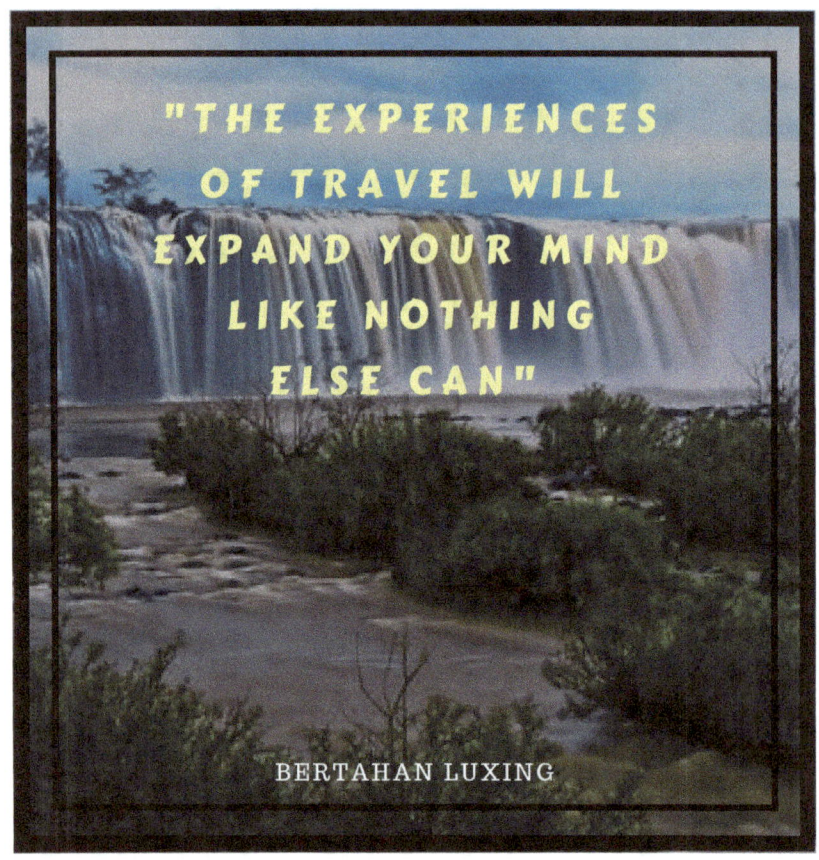

The experiences of travel will expand your mind like nothing else can.

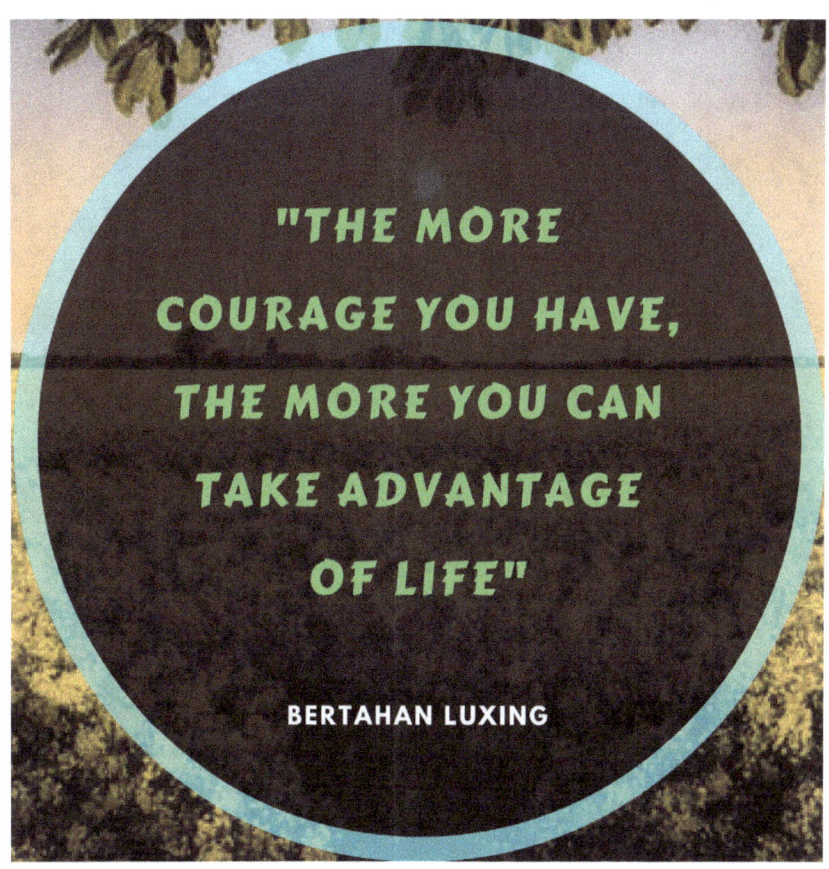

The more courage you have, the more you can take advantage of life.

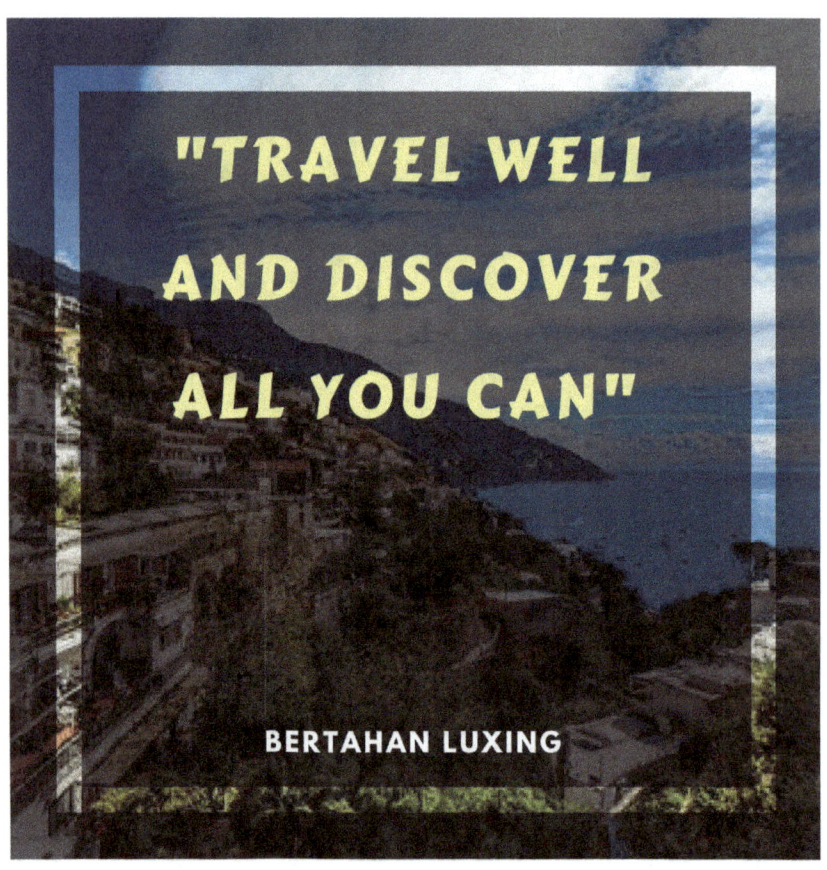

Travel well and discover all you can.

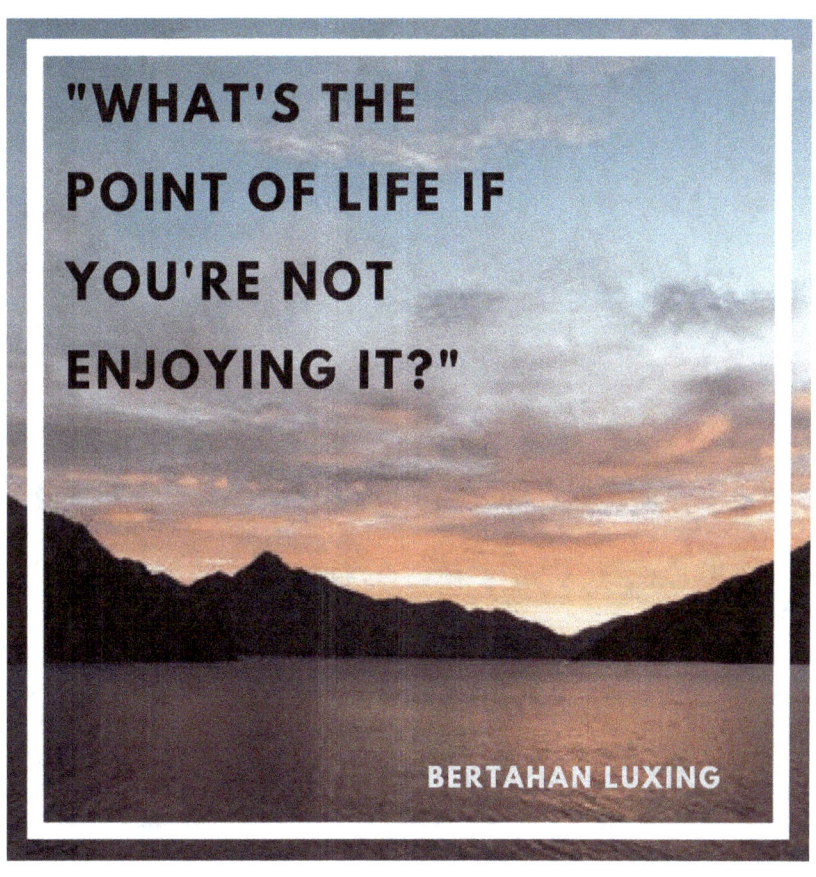

What's the point of life if you're not enjoying it?

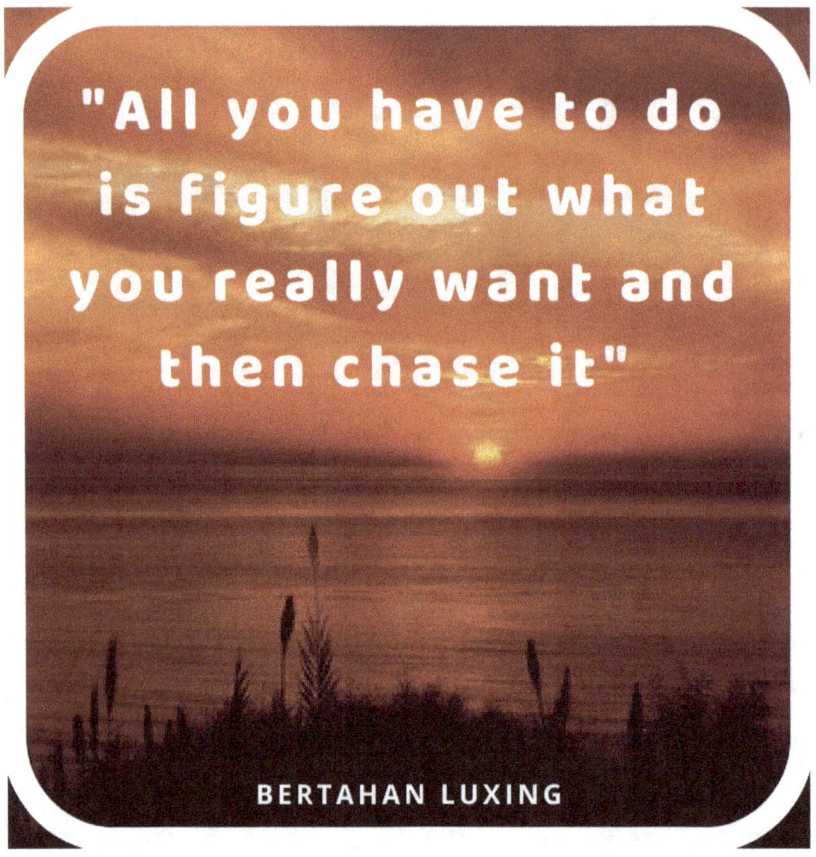

All you have to do is figure out what you really want and then chase it.

Break out of the prison in your mind. Explore out of your comfort zone. Travel.

If you can dream it, you can do it. All you need is the will.

The less 'stuff' you have, material or otherwise, the more freedom you will have.

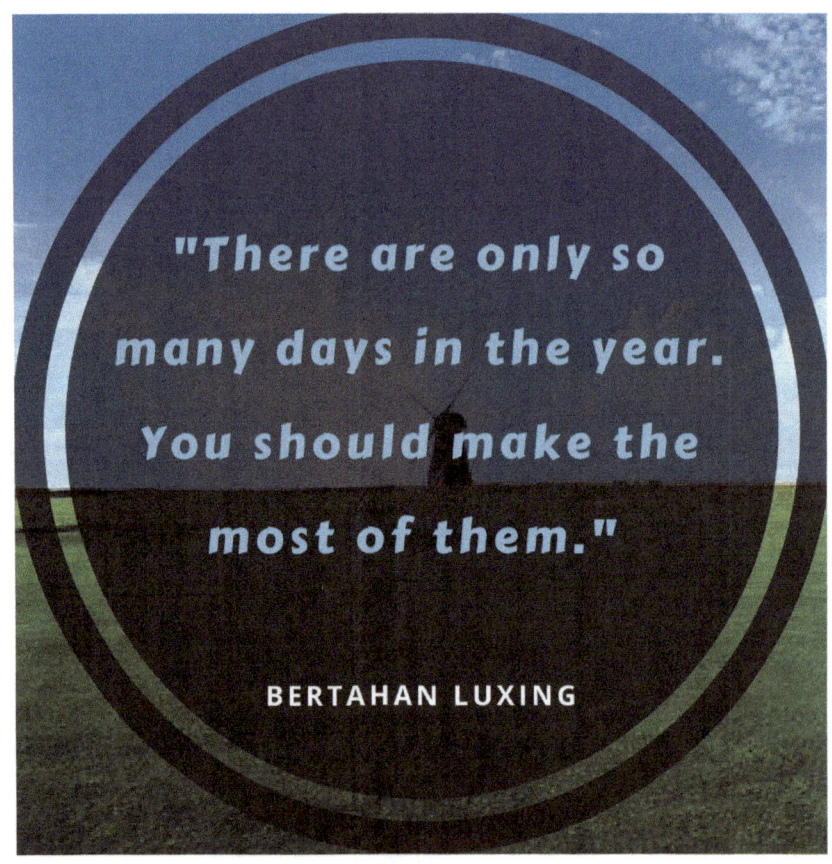

There are only so many days in the year. You should make the most of them.

Travel keeps the mind young and fresh – like sudoku but with more world.

You don't need to know exactly where you are going before you start to move.

All the best things I've discovered have been while I'm getting lost.

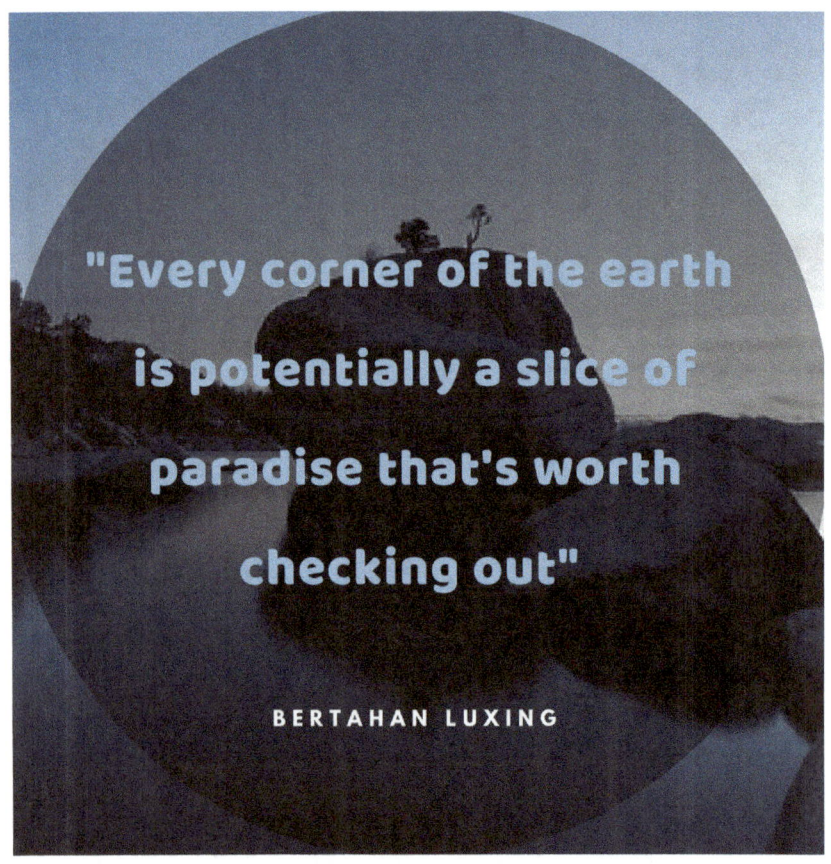

Every corner of the earth is potentially a slice of paradise that's worth checking out.

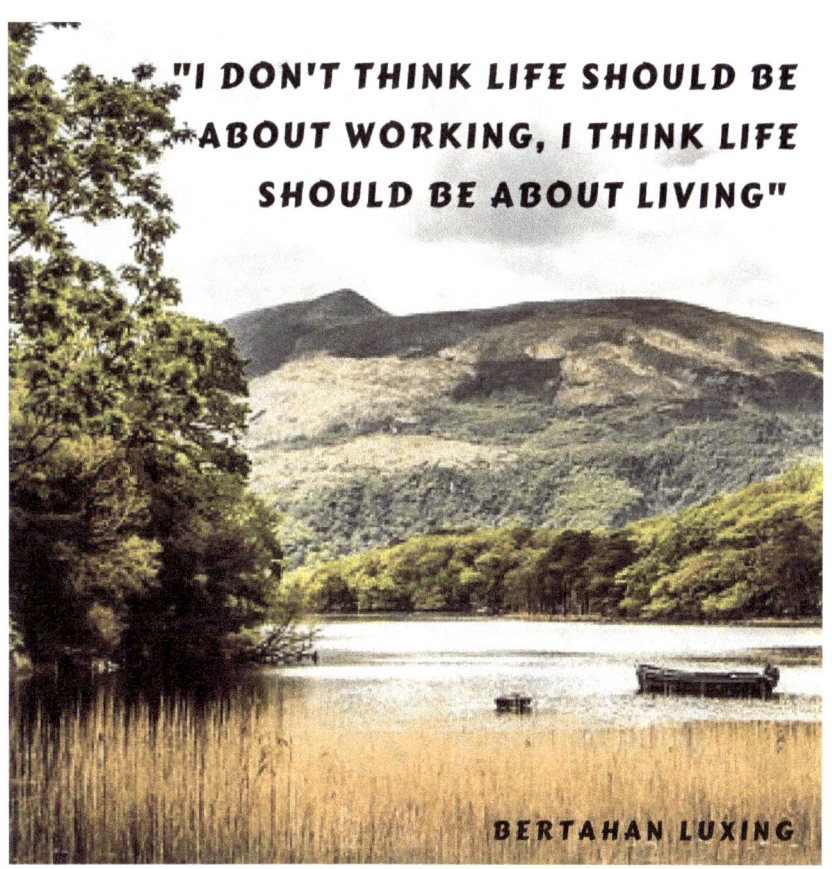

I don't think life should be about working, I think life should be about living.

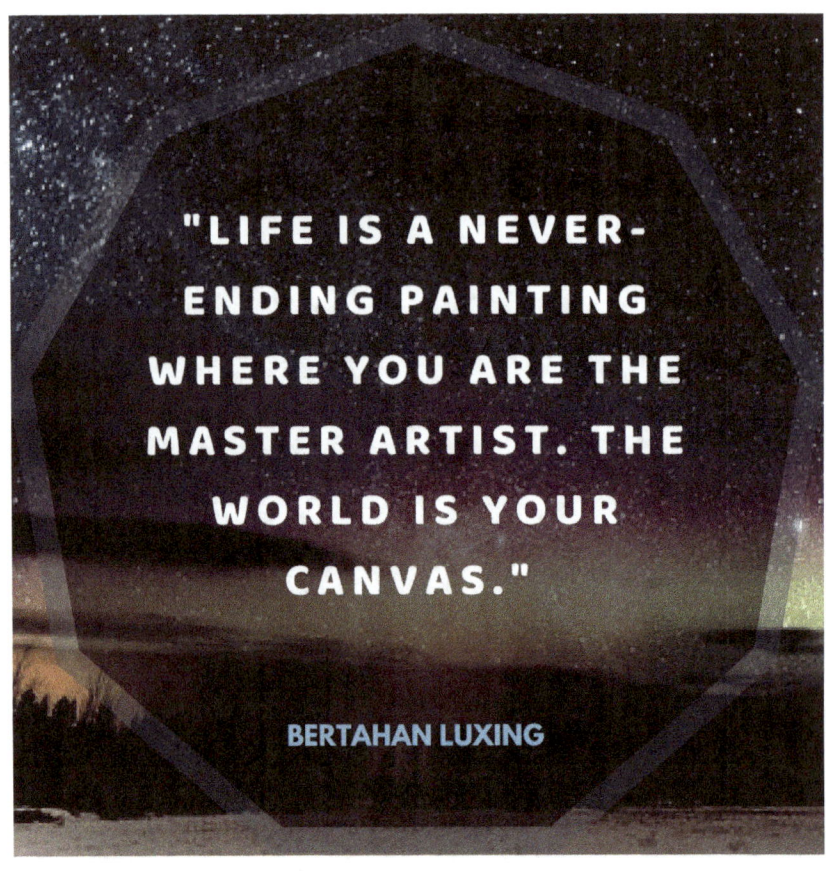

Life is a never-ending painting where you are the master artist. The world is your canvas.

Make the most out of the life you've got. Who knows if we get another chance.

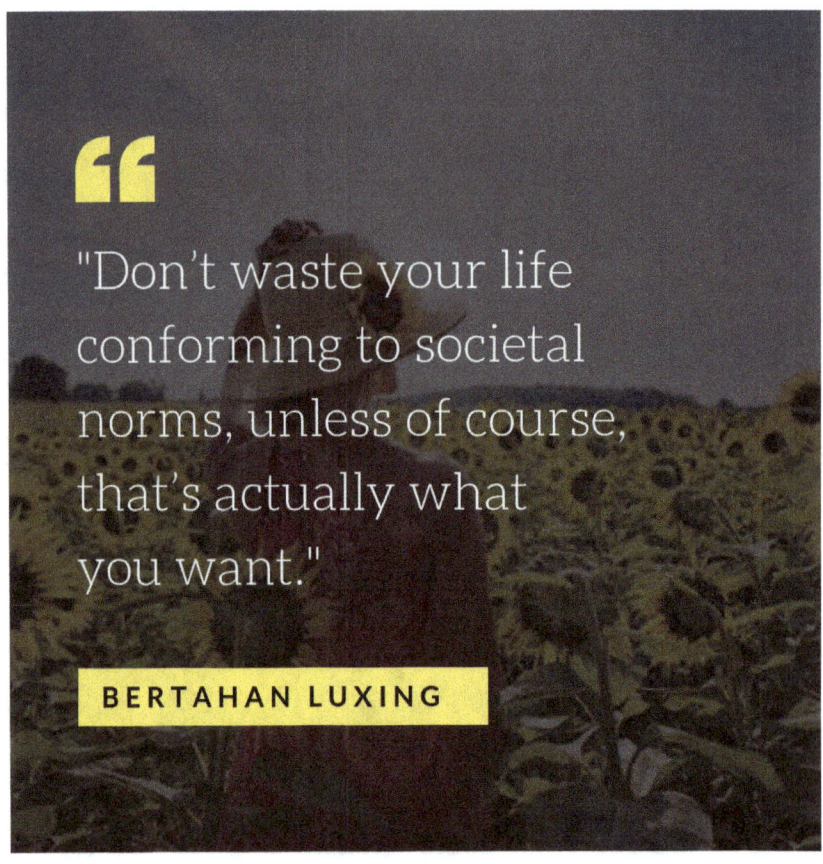

Don't waste your life conforming to societal norms, unless of course, that's actually what you want.

Not only will you discover amazing places, you will also discover yourself. That is the true beauty of travel.

Travel so one day you won't be saying 'I wish I had traveled more'.

Dare to dream, then dare to live that dream.

Don't get so caught up in a societal life that you forget to do the things you want.

Don't just exist, live. Travel.

Go make your memories, anywhere and everywhere.

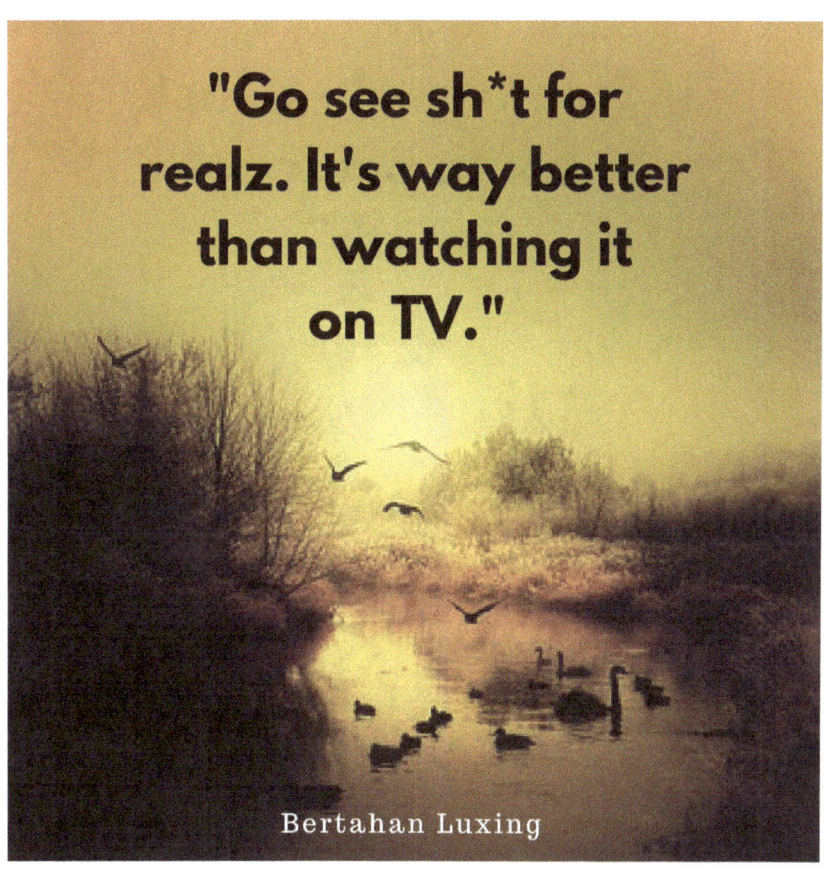

*Go see sh*t for realz. It's way better than watching it on TV.*

Solo travel – a fast track to personal growth.

The only real failure in life is if you didn't at least try to live the one you dreamed of.

Traveling will keep you young.

Unlike trees, we can move, travel, explore. What would the trees think if we wasted these gifts?

What life do you dream of?

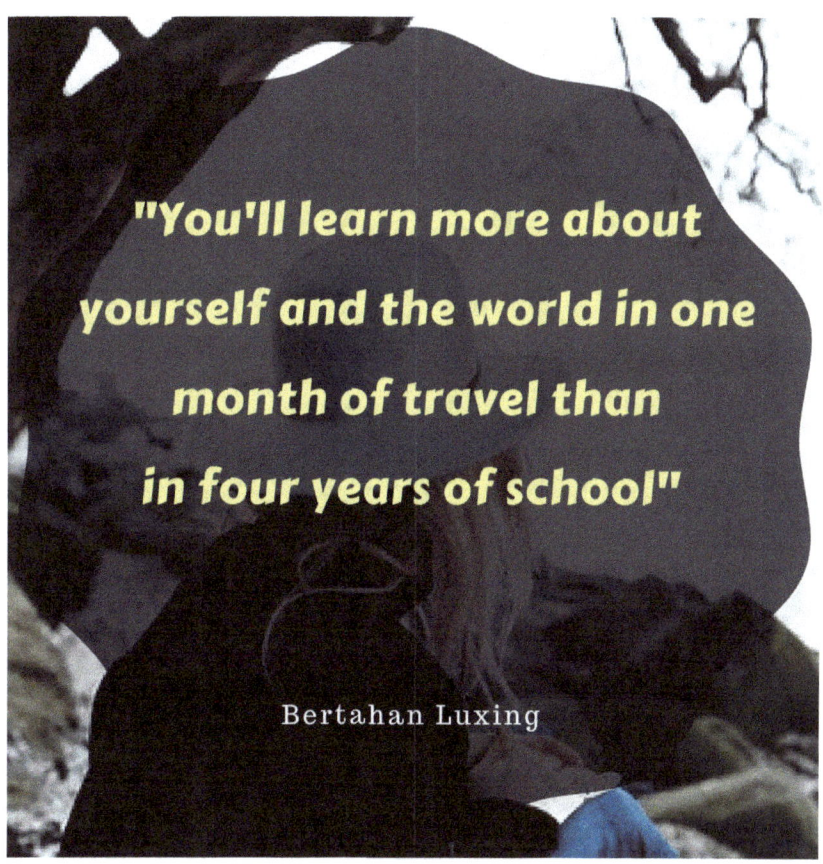

You'll learn more about yourself and the world in one month of travel than in four years of school.

Create the awesome life you want, one adventure at a time.

Focus on the outcome, not the obstacles.

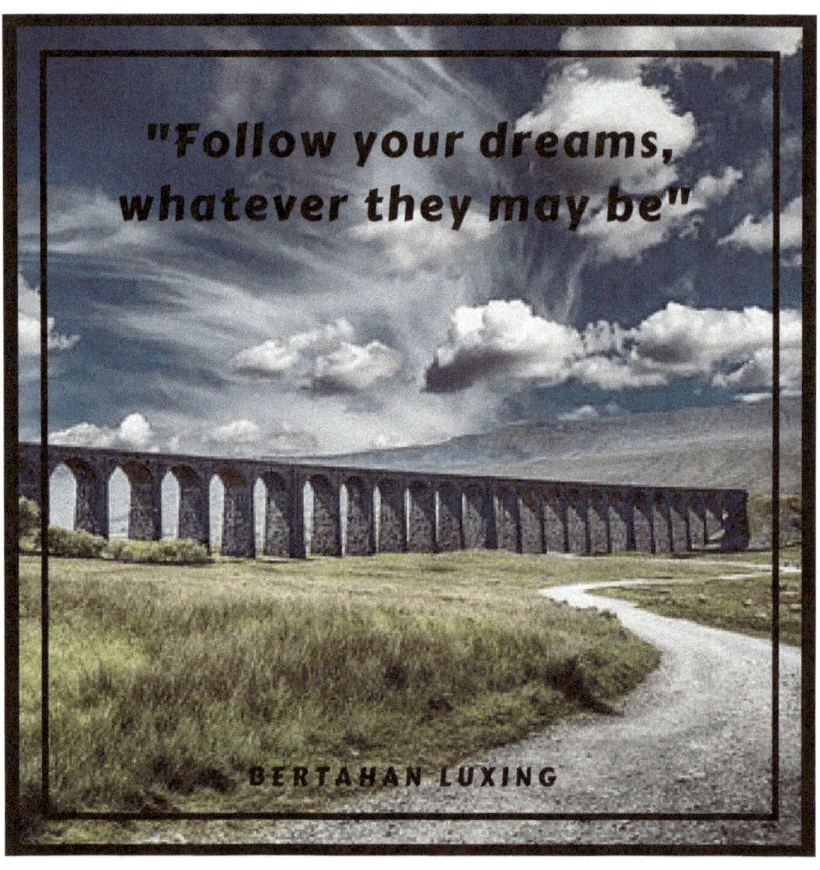

Follow your dreams, whatever they may be.

Never stop dreaming. The more you dream it, the more likely it will come true.

Step out the door and let life sweep you away.

The little things in life often bring the most joy. Traveling will allow you to see much more of those little things.

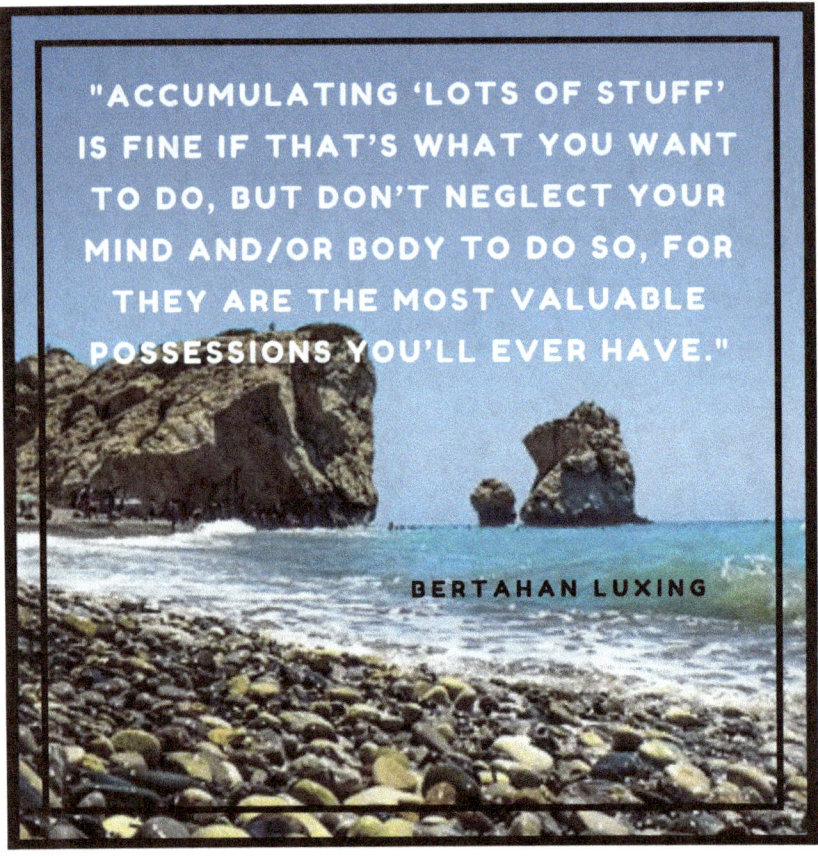

Accumulating 'lots of stuff' is fine if that's what you want to do, but don't neglect your mind and/or body to do so, for they are the most valuable possessions you'll ever have.

Create the 'you' you want to be.

Getting lost may be one of the best ways to travel.

It's all too easy to have life pass you by via routine and the conformity of social norms.

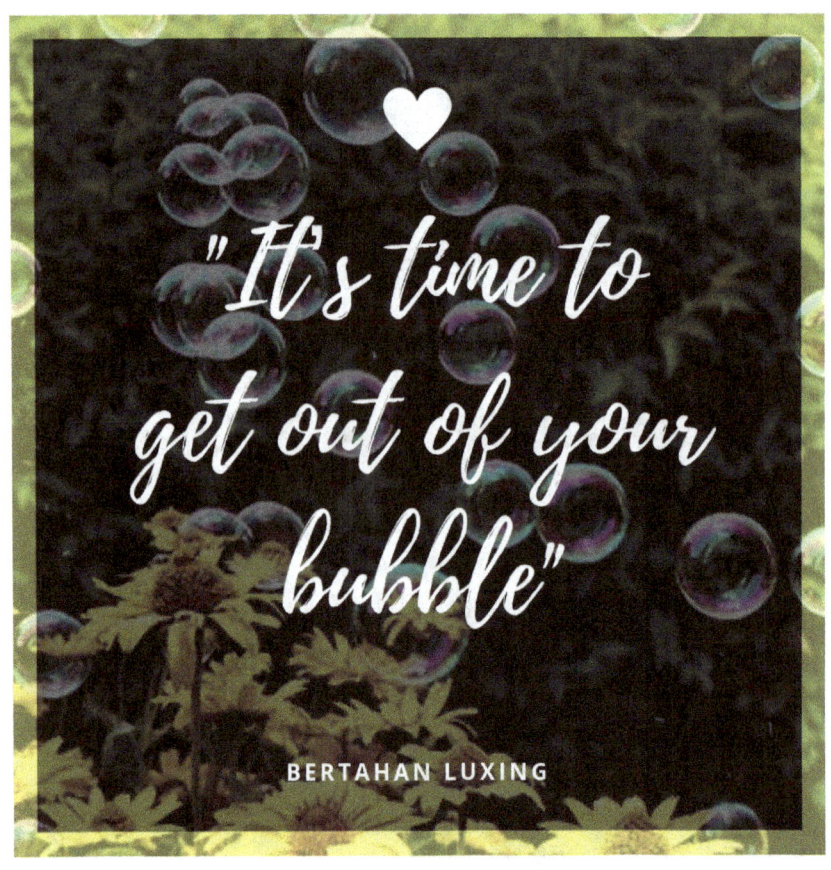

It's time to get out of your bubble.

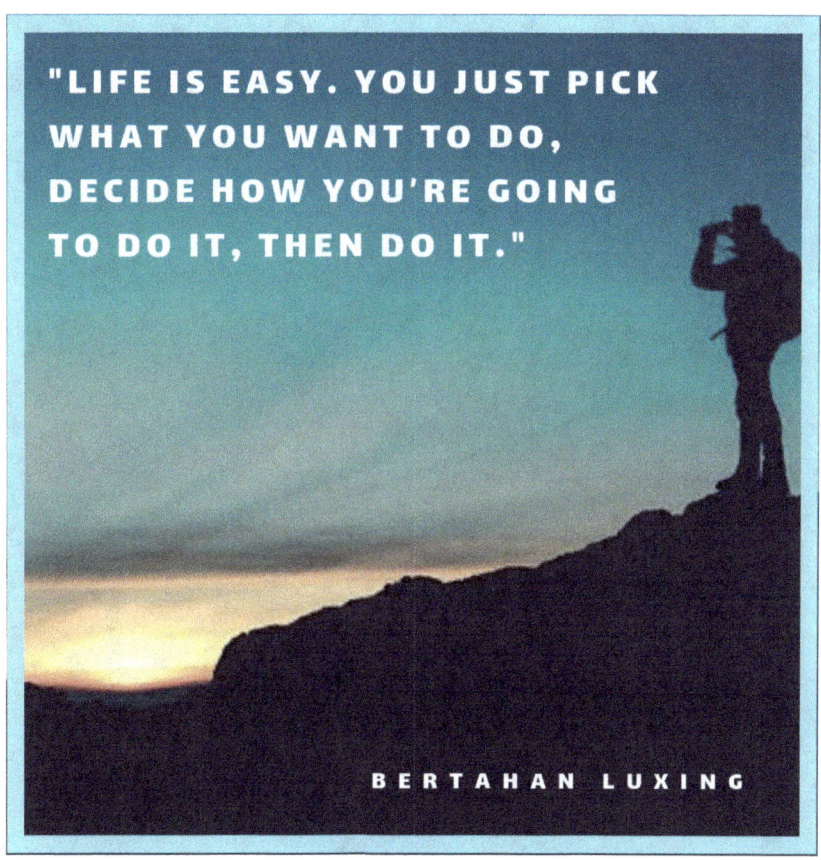

Life is easy. You just pick what you want to do, decide how you're going to do it, then do it.

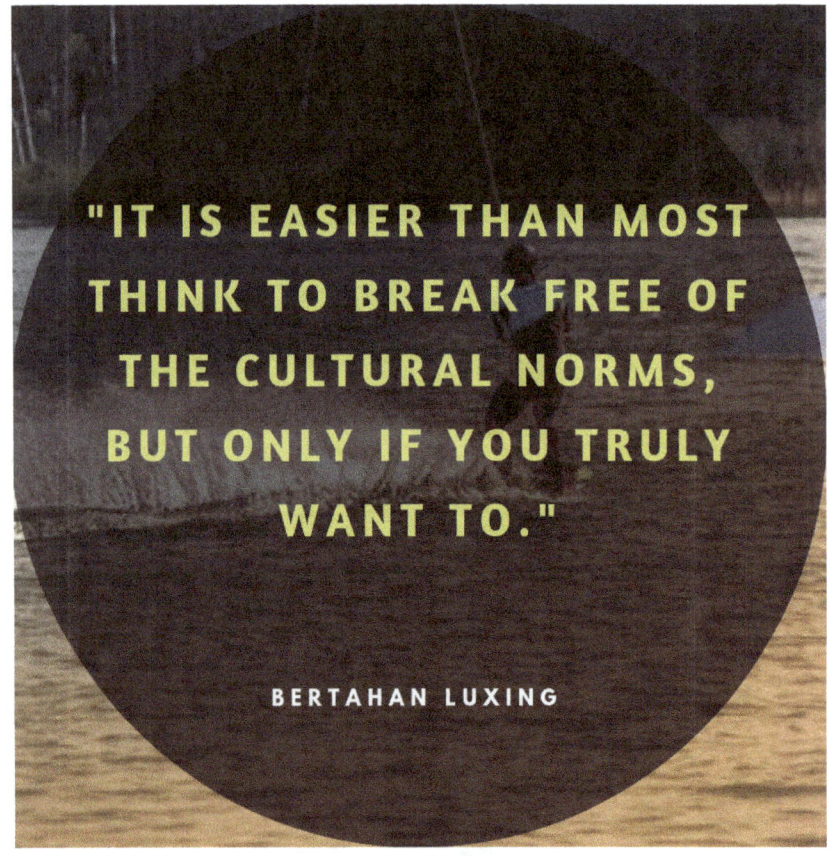

It's easier than most think to break free of the cultural norms, but only if you truly want to.

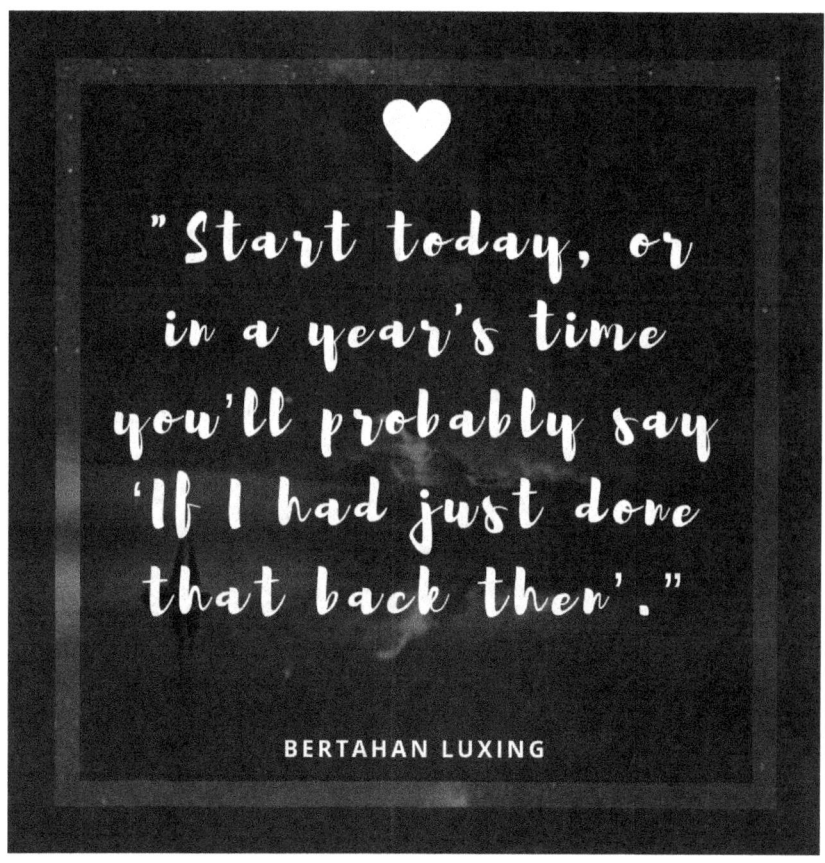

Start today, or in a year's time you'll probably say 'If I had just done that back then'.

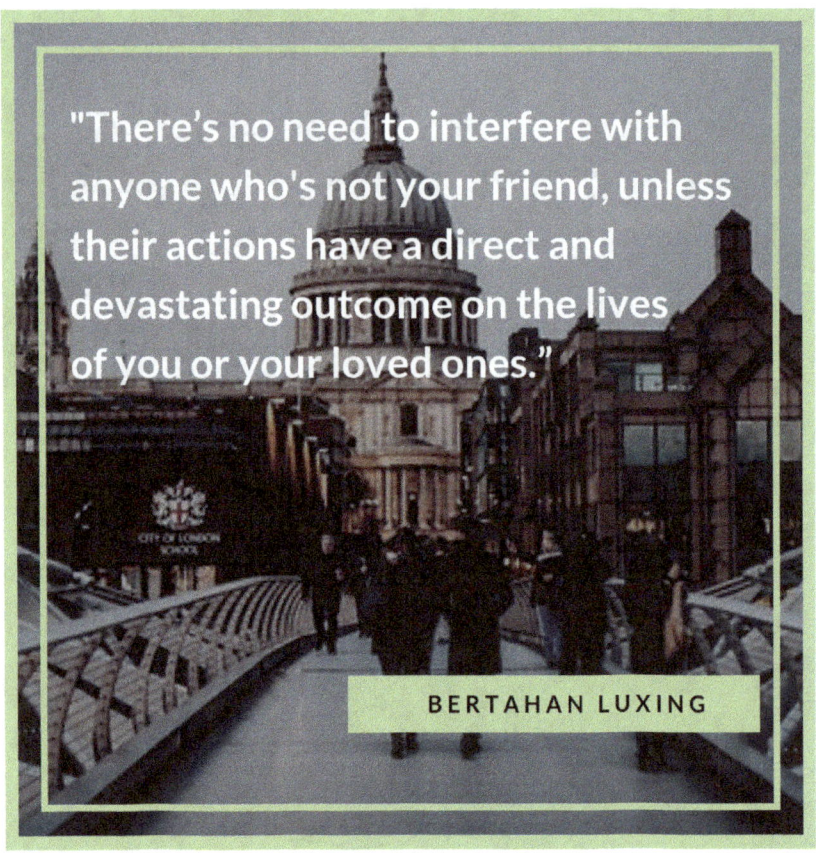

There's no need to interfere with anyone who's not your friend, unless their actions have a direct and devastating outcome on the lives of you or your loved ones.

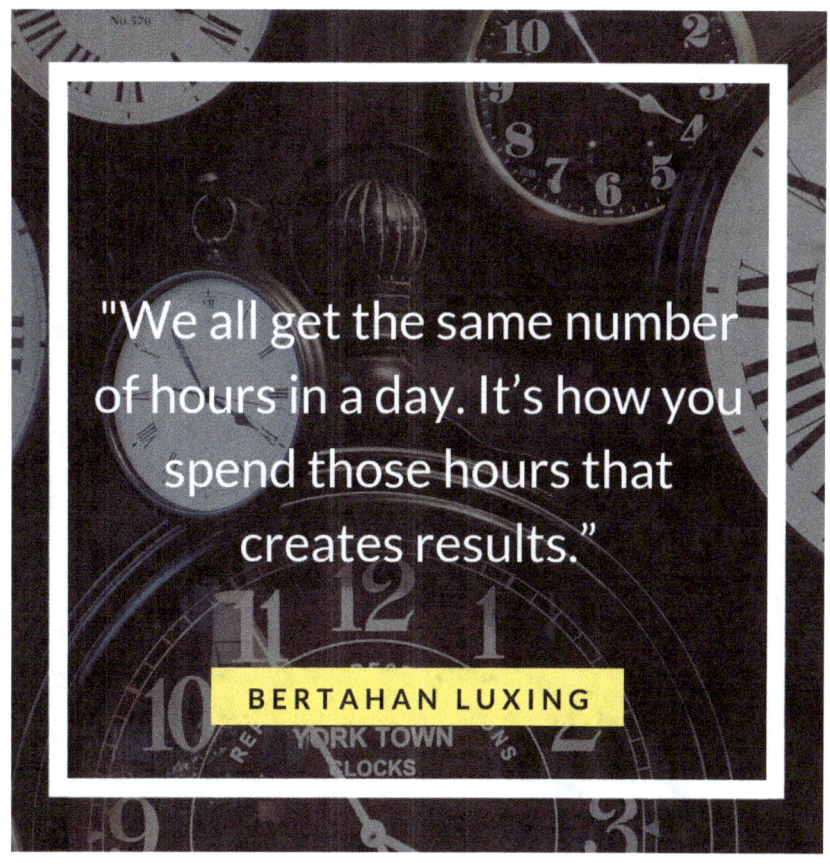

We all get the same number of hours in a day. It's how you spend those hours that creates results.

Don't let your attachment of 'stuff' hold you back, material or otherwise. Less is more, always.

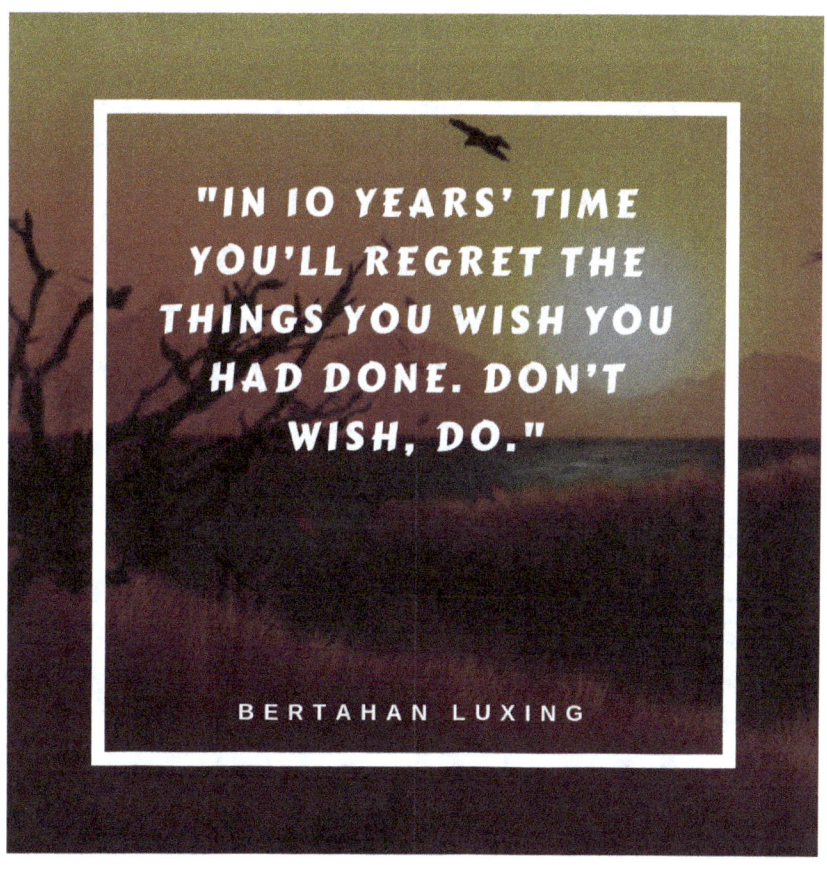

In 10 years' time you'll regret the things you wish you had done. Don't wish, do.

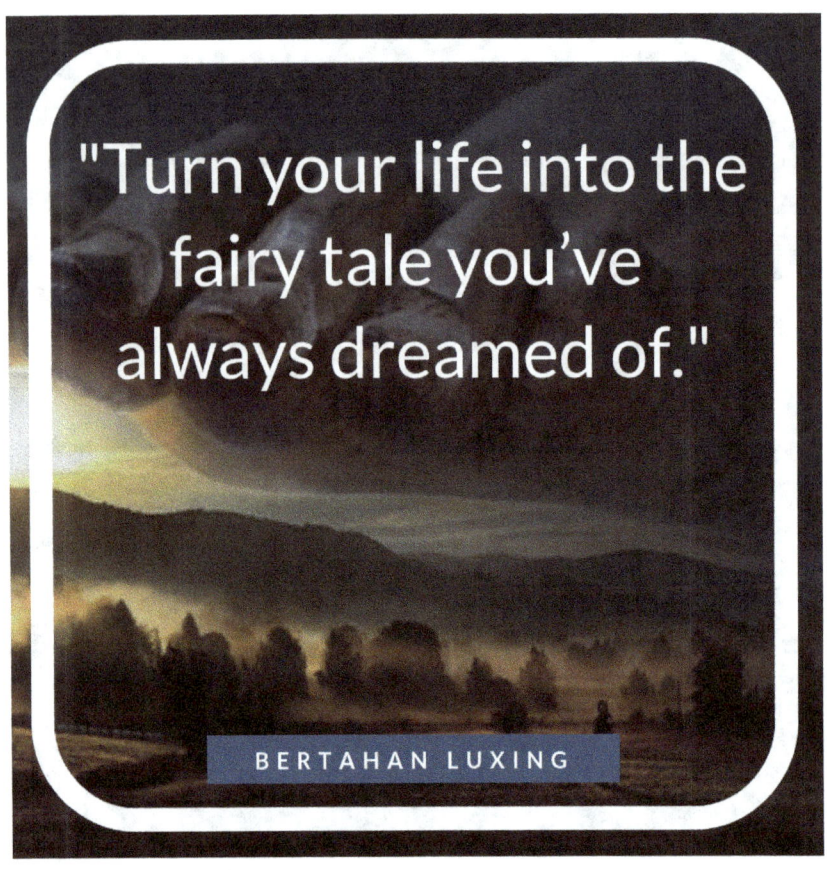

Turn your life into the fairy tale you've always dreamed of.

Travel and you are guaranteed to discover strengths you never knew you had.

Usually if you truly believe you can do it, then you can.

Dear Reader,

Thank you for reading **The Inspirational Travel Quotes Book.**

If you enjoyed this book, please leave a review where you bought it. It helps more than most people think.

Thanks again for your support,

Aventuras De Viaje, Author.

AUTHOR RECOMMENDATIONS

Save Big on Your Next Travel Adventure

If your planning to travel you need this book, because everyone likes getting the best deal!

Get it now.

www.SurvivalFitnessPlan.com/Budget-Travel

Discover How to Use Yoga as Medicine

Add this book to your collection, because with it you can use yoga to heal your mind, body, and spirit.

Get it now.

www.SurvivalFitnessPlan.com/Curing-Yoga

ABOUT THE AUTHOR

Aventuras has 3 passions: travel, writing, and self-improvement.

Combining these 3 things Miss Viaje spends her time traveling the world and learning about all the things she loves.

She takes what she learns and shares it with the world through her books.

www.SurvivalFitnessPlan.com

- facebook.com/SurvivalFitnessPlan
- twitter.com/Survival_Fitnes
- pinterest.com/survivalfitnes
- goodreads.com/MissAventurasDeViaje
- bookbub.com/authors/aventuras-de-viaje
- amazon.com/author/aventuras

www.ingramcontent.com/pod-product-compliance
Lightning Source LLC
Chambersburg PA
CBHW071449080526
44587CB00014B/2052